How Shall We Witness?

How Shall We Witness?

Faithful Evangelism in a Reformed Tradition

Milton J Coalter and Virgil Cruz
editors

 Westminster John Knox Press
Louisville, Kentucky

© 1995 Westminster John Knox Press

Scripture quotations from the New Revised Standard Version of the Bible are copyright © 1989 by the Division of Christian Education of the National Council of the Churches of Christ in the U.S.A. and are used by permission.

Book and cover design by Drew Stevens

Cover illustration: Camp Meeting, *lithograph by Kennedy & Lucas after painting by A. Rider, c. 1835. Courtesy of The New-York Historical Society.*

First edition

Published by Westminster John Knox Press
Louisville, Kentucky

This book is printed on acid-free paper that meets the American National Standards Institute Z39.48 standard. ∞

PRINTED IN THE UNITED STATES OF AMERICA

95 96 97 98 99 00 01 02 03 04 — 10 9 8 7 6 5 4 3 2 1

Library of Congress Cataloging-in-Publication Data

How shall we witness? : faithful evangelism in a Reformed tradition /
    Milton J Coalter, Virgil Cruz, editors. — 1st ed.
        p.   cm.
    Papers originally presented at a conference sponsored by Louisville
Presbyterian Theological Seminary, Mar. 1993.
    ISBN 0-664-25575-2 (alk. paper)
    1. Evangelistic work—Congresses.   2. Presbyterian Church—
Membership—Congresses.   3. Reformed Church—Membership—Congresses.
I. Coalter, Milton J. II. Cruz, Virgil. III. Louisville Presbyterian Theological
Seminary.
BV3790.H756   1995
269'.2'08825—dc20   94-36762

To Lin and Margot

Contents

Acknowledgments

A book on faithful witness to the Word Incarnate demands a faithful witness to all who midwifed this volume's incarnation. The number of midwives to this project is legion, but some deserve special note.

Without the collaboration of our colleagues John M. Mulder and Louis B. Weeks this study would never have been conceived. Moreover, the financial support of the Pew Charitable Trusts and the encouragement of Joel A. Carpenter, the director of the Pew Charitable Trusts' Religion Program, allowed the seedling idea of this research to find form, first as a conference and now as a book.

We are also deeply thankful for William Abraham, Joanna Adams, William J. Carl, Timothy L. Croft, James Cushman, Arlo Duba, Charles W. Forman, Sarah M. Foulger, Donald Gowan, John R. Hendrick, Ben Campbell Johnson, Robert Jones, Clifton Kirkpatrick, Sang Lee, Marcia C. Myers, Earl Palmer, Dale W. Patterson, Amy Plantinga Pauw, Ronald Peters, Andrea Pfaff, Syngman Rhee, Joyce Tucker, and Rebecca Weaver. These individuals elevated the level of conversation about outreach at the Faithful Witness Conference held at Louisville Presbyterian Theological Seminary, Louisville, Kentucky, in March 1993, and their insightful papers or critiques expanded the vision of responsible contemporary witness found in these essays.

Contributors

Edith L. Blumhofer is associate professor of history and director of the Institute for the Study of American Evangelicals at Wheaton College, Wheaton, Illinois. Some of her more recent publications include *Aimee Semple McPherson* and *Modern Christian Revivals,* the latter co-edited with Randall Balmer.

Milton J Coalter is the library director and professor of bibliography and research at Louisville Presbyterian Theological Seminary. He is also a board member of the Louisville Institute for the Study of Protestantism and American Culture in Louisville, Kentucky.

Virgil Cruz is professor of New Testament at Louisville Presbyterian Theological Seminary in Louisville, Kentucky, and has served as president for one term and board member of Presbyterians for Renewal since its conception.

Dawn DeVries is associate professor of church history at McCormick Theological Seminary in Chicago. She previously taught at San Francisco Theological Seminary.

Catherine Gunsalus González is professor of church history at Columbia Theological Seminary in Decatur, Georgia. With Justo L. González, she has authored *Liberating Preaching* and *Visions at Patmos.*

Darrell L. Guder is professor of global mission and evangelism at Louisville Presbyterian Theological Seminary and currently is a leader in the Gospel and Culture Network.

David C. Hester is professor of Christian education at Louisville Presbyterian Theological Seminary. He is the author of numerous scholarly articles as well as curriculum materials in the Presbyterian and Reformed Educational Ministries.

Louis B. Weeks is president of Union Theological Seminary in Richmond, Virginia, and a board member of the Louisville Institute for the Study of Protestantism and American Culture. He co-edited a seven-volume series on American Presbyterianism, titled The Presbyterian Presence: The Twentieth-Century Experience, with Milton J Coalter and John M. Mulder.

Ronald C. White, Jr., is a lecturer in history at the University of California at Los Angeles and a research scholar at the Huntington Library. His most recent publication is *Liberty and Justice for All: Racial Reform and the Social Gospel.*

Albert Curry Winn is president emeritus and professor emeritus of systematic theology at Louisville Presbyterian Theological Seminary. He is also a former Moderator of the Presbyterian Church in the U.S.

Introduction

MILTON J COALTER

The story of Reformed evangelism is, in one sense, a common tale. It is the account of yet one more Christian family of disciples seeking to heed Christ's commission to witness in and to the world. However, Reformed Christians' historic quest for a faithful witness has been complex, filled with energetic proclamation and service, false starts, theological controversies, and experimentation. This complexity is significant because it mirrors the sources of past and present ambiguity and debate about evangelism experienced elsewhere in the Christian community.

Changing times have regularly demanded adaptations of Reformed witness. In order to address new social and religious situations, Reformed Christians, like other Christian communions, have repeatedly experimented with various forms of outreach.

At the same time, they have also assumed that scripture's revelation of Christ as *the* "faithful witness" provides his disciples with a clear definition of what faithful outreach is and should be. Consequently, with each modification of their evangelistic practice, Reformed communions have struggled to determine not only which evangelistic methods fit the times but also which forms of witness continue true to the scriptural vision of Christian discipleship.

In some instances, this constant questioning of evangelistic practice has produced a healthy wariness toward techniques that simplistically equated membership growth with successful outreach. In other cases, conflicts over the meaning and methods of faithful witness have exaggerated Reformed reservations in ways that, at best, frustrated a vigorous and timely witness in word and deed or, at worst, questioned evangelism's place among the tasks of Christian discipleship.

Today, Reformed concerns about evangelism are a mixture of sincere theological scruples and misguided inhibitions about the evangelistic task. The former can continue to instruct Christian witness by providing both direction and focus. The latter only serve to confuse and to hinder needlessly disciples' participation in outreach.

The eight essays in this book are the result of a three-year research effort to address current Christian ambivalence about the church's evangelistic mission. They recall the complicated search for a faithful Reformed witness, and they clarify the theological visions that have motivated and undergirded that pursuit. This study of the theology and history of Reformed evangelism has been coordinated at Louisville Presbyterian Theological Seminary and funded by the Pew Charitable Trusts. Along with several other research papers, early versions of these essays were first presented at a March 1993 conference titled Faithful Witness.[1]

More conversation and study are needed to accomplish even the limited task of these essays and the conference that spawned them. This volume certainly does not cover the topics comprehensively. It focuses on the Reformed tradition, which is only one theological family in the larger body of Christ. It also gives special attention to the Presbyterian experience in America as a case study of the greater Reformed community, a fellowship of communions that now encompasses almost two hundred denominational bodies across the globe. Nevertheless, these essays are an invitation to a much-needed conversation about the legitimate and unjustified reservations about evangelism that many contemporary Christians express.

With this goal in mind, the volume is divided into three parts. The first considers the theology of outreach; the second provides a case history of Reformed involvement in witness; and the third suggests pivotal concerns that can guide and motivate the future practice of evangelism.

The first section, which lays a theological and educational foundation for outreach, begins with a discussion by Albert Curry Winn of the content of witness. Winn asks: Just what is the gospel of Jesus Christ? What has the Christian "good news" been in different stages of the church's development, and what remains "good" and "news" even today? During the nineteenth century, American

Protestant churches attempted to instill a distinctly Christian ethos into American life. In the words of the historian Robert Handy, their aim was to create a "Christian America." Their goal was accomplished only in part, and it has had an ironic consequence. Today American culture, which presumes to be well acquainted with Christianity, questions whether there is much good or news still to be gleaned from its old-time religion.

Winn addresses this challenge first by humbly acknowledging several ways in which Reformed theology and practice have obscured key elements in the New Testament gospel. However, he goes further to note three factors that promise to make the good news new again for North American and European societies. Winn suggests that twentieth-century theologies like those of Karl Barth and Jürgen Moltmann recast Reformed Christian identity in the hope and witness of the scriptural good news. Likewise, the collapse of European and North American domination over Christianity's institutional definitions of the gospel message plus the rise of cross-cultural conversation among indigenous Christian communities around the world can free North American and European Christians to listen to other disciple communities' witness. This shift in the flow of Christian conversation allows historic missionary communions to learn from those to whom they once witnessed. In the process, they can rediscover aspects of the good news forgotten or obscured by their particular religious experience and culture.

Dawn DeVries follows Winn with a consideration of the conversion experience. In the American setting, conversion has become for many Christians the singular goal of an evangelistic mission. In contrast, DeVries shows that the inclination of Reformed Christians has been to moderate the common emphasis on conversion's individual and once-for-all-time character. Reformed communions have regarded conversion as but one step in two larger processes on the path of discipleship. Conversion from a Reformed perspective is as much a communal event as an individual one since it culminates in the individual's incorporation into the communion of Christ's followers. Conversion also launches the Christian on a lifelong process of regeneration and growth in perfecting one's faith and witness. For this reason, responsible Reformed evangelism has resisted focusing its energies exclusively on the conversion event. Instead, it has aimed its work more broadly at facilitating all areas of Christian maturation.

This growth in faith and witness is the topic of David Hester's essay. Evangelism is most frequently identified with the act of bringing converts to Christ. Yet Reformed theology has insisted that the church does not convert anyone. God alone transforms the human heart. The church only cooperates in this transformation by nurturing the witness of Christ's disciples. Recognizing this fundamental conviction, Hester considers the church's evangelistic role in maturing Christians' understanding of the gospel so that they may embody it faithfully. Hester contends that the church first nourishes witnesses, who are young in the faith, by instilling a sense of their belonging in communion with one another under God and teaching them to discern the signs of God's continued, active presence throughout creation.

The church can then foster further maturation by helping members rethink the traditions that they have received from past disciples in the light of new social contexts and the Christian faith revealed in scripture. This contributes to their outreach truthfully reflecting the profundity of the revelation in a contemporary embodiment of voice and service.

Finally, Hester insists that Reformed communions must propel Christ's witnesses into the public arena where they cooperate with the divine, the church community, and non-Christians in promoting justice, love, and mercy among individuals and social structures.

These theological studies of Reformed evangelism are followed by a second group of essays that considers the historical development of Reformed outreach, particularly as it was exemplified in the American Presbyterian experience. They examine how the methods and emphases of Reformed evangelism adapted to the church's changing environment. They also describe the numerous debates and conflicts about the scriptural borders of a faithful witness that these shifts occasioned.

Addressing the period from the Reformation to the Wesleyan movement of the eighteenth century, Catherine González investigates the vital concern of early Reformation leaders for some forms of evangelism and their relative apathy toward others. The earliest Protestant Reformers were primarily interested in converting fellow Christians to a scriptural piety and church life cleansed of what they considered the superstition and error of the medieval church. Their involvement in evangelism in this regard was energetic. But their vision of outreach only in the rarest instances stretched beyond the confines of European Christendom.

Early Reformed leaders also emphasized both predestination and God's sovereignty. This introduced into the tradition a sense that disciples' witness was at best a secondary factor in the evangelization of the world.

Later Reformed groups, like the English Puritans, were more aware of the world beyond established European Christianity, and they were vitally interested in pastorally assisting sin-sick souls in their search for the trustworthy path to salvation. As a result, missions to the unconverted world beyond Christendom assumed a higher profile in Reformed circles. The conversion experience and the steps to it received more attention than ever before. The tradition also began to stress the clergy's responsibility to facilitate such personal transformation by witnessing "in season," that is, directing their spiritual oversight and preaching to the particular stages in the process of conversion where their parishioners' hearts resided.

Edith Blumhofer next studies the adjustments required of Reformed communions as their members moved to the New World. Blumhofer notes that Reformed Christians adapted their Old World evangelistic practice to their altered situation in several ways. Presbyterians adapted Scottish and Scots-Irish communion practices to promote revivals. They developed missions to Native Americans, to African Americans, and later to the entire world, and they created new institutional forms of outreach like the benevolent societies of the early nineteenth century and the 1801 Plan of Union between Presbyterians and Congregationalists.

These adaptations generated controversy in three areas. First, old Reformed reservations were raised about the limited role that humans can play in their own spiritual transformation or in that of others. This led significant portions of the Presbyterian community to question the practice and theology of the First and Second Great Awakening revivals. Second, scruples about revivalists' manipulation of emotions and their focus on conversion split the Presbyterian Church on two separate occasions. Third, Presbyterians disputed the wisdom of ecumenical evangelistic cooperation. Benevolent societies and the 1801 Plan of Union were believed by some to undermine theological purity or to suggest that evangelism is a voluntary choice of individuals rather than the work of all church members.

Interestingly enough, no party in any of these disputes questioned evangelism's place at the heart of Christian discipleship. Furthermore, all assumed that evangelism and mission were synonymous or, at the very least, coterminous.

This nineteenth-century consensus did not endure the twentieth century. The essays by Louis Weeks and Ronald White explain why. Both studies demonstrate that the meaning of evangelism has shrunk even as the definition of mission has expanded. American denominations adopted the corporate bureaucratic structure of modern business during the twentieth century. As a result, evangelism became one among many program areas of the church's mission rather than the motivating principle behind mission. Also, evangelism became more closely identified with verbal proclamation for the purpose of converting individuals to the Christian faith. This stands in stark contrast with earlier Reformed insistence on a full-bodied witness of word and service in support of transforming individuals and social institutions.

These developments have made evangelism a "line in the sand" between Christians instead of a motivating force propelling them to a comprehensive witness. Some church leaders emphasize the necessity of voiced declarations of the Christian gospel and verbal invitations into Christian communion. Others stress the value of exemplary service to Christlike justice and love in society. The unfortunate consequence of this debate is that too often both contingents eye their counterpart's approach with suspicion at best, and at worst regard it as a questionable competitor for the church community's attention.

This conflict has been debilitating for all concerned. It has divided the church's evangelistic energies. It has reversed evangelism's natural outward orientation by focusing the community's attention on an internecine controversy. But most of all, it has left large numbers of Christians bewildered about their responsibility as witnesses. Moreover, they do not understand, or in some cases have never heard, the complex constellation of scriptural warrant and restraint that channeled earlier Reformed witness.

Despite recent efforts to heal this impoverishing division of word and deed, it persists, and in a certain sense, it has been exacerbated by the additional question of pluralism. The presence of a plurality of races, religions, and cultural or ethnic backgrounds is not new to the world, to the United States, or to the biblical faith. Likewise, the church has long experience with efforts to express the Christian faith in diverse ways.

Ecclesiastical sanction for disparate theological views and practice in the church and the society has, however, been extended dramatically during the latter half of the twentieth century. For some Christians, this new latitude for pluralism is troubling because they fear that it leaves Christians with little in common to proclaim collectively. For others, the evangelistic consequence of pluralism simply leaves them confused. And for still others, the recent acknowledgment of pluralism is welcomed, but it makes evangelism something of an embarrassment. If evangelism's goal is to persuade the whole world that Jesus Christ is "the way, and the truth, and the life," then they ask, Is it not out of step with the present times when differences are tolerated and honored?

Puzzled as to how this quandary might be resolved, grassroots church people exhibit a mixed mind regarding evangelism. On the one hand, they continue to insist that evangelism must remain high in their denominations' priorities because the call to witness is clearly proclaimed in scripture. On the other hand, they personally avoid getting involved in evangelism. Such crippling ambiguity calls for the Christian community to reconsider its theology and practice of witness much as previous generations have done in the light of changing conditions.

The last section in this volume begins this work as Darrell Guder attempts to locate the pivotal concerns in Reformed history and theology that might ground a rethinking of contemporary witness. Guder suggests that Reformed evangelism is confused by the church community's own lack of clarity on three major issues: Who is Jesus Christ? How is witness to Christ in word and service integrated? Where does the church's primary mission lie? Guder insists that any resolution of this confusion requires the fundamental recognition that faithful witness should not be informed by the church's need for institutional survival. Rather it finds its direction from the invigorating discovery of good news for private and public human life found uniquely in Jesus Christ. In Christ the church finds embodied the *missio Dei* (the mission of God) to create *koinōnia* (community) through both *kērygma* (the good news of salvation proclaimed) and *diakonia* (the good news of salvation enacted through service).

Guder's essay does not speak for the other authors represented here, but it builds on their work and that of other researchers reported at the Faithful Witness Conference mentioned earlier in this introduction.

At the conclusion of that conference, as leaders discussed the study's implications for evangelism, Isaac Fokuo, a pastor from Ghana, stood to remark, "But you have not spoken enough about the Holy Spirit!" This perceptive observation should be highlighted at the beginning of these essays about the church's evangelism. Before any conversation about human disciples' role in witness, the necessity of the Holy Spirit must be affirmed. Christian witness is ultimately prompted, sustained, and efficacious only with the help of the Holy Spirit. The church cannot direct the Spirit's action. The Spirit of God moves like the wind where it wills. But the church can seek prayerfully the Spirit's guidance, first, in discerning where the Spirit is active and, second, in determining appropriate ways to cooperate with the Spirit's birthing new life throughout the creation.

The authors in this volume wish in no way to obscure the priority of the Holy Spirit in Christian witness. But they do hope to illuminate better the precise character of Christian disciples' collaboration with the Spirit in the presentation of a truly faithful witness.

NOTE

1. Papers presented at the Faithful Witness Conference but not published in this volume are available from Milton J Coalter, Louisville Presbyterian Theological Seminary, 1044 Alta Vista Road, Louisville, KY 40205.

Part 1. Theological Foundations
for Witness

1. What Is the Gospel?

ALBERT CURRY WINN

What is the gospel? It seems a simple question until we ponder it. Then its profundity and its relevance to the central concern of this book become evident.[1] After all, evangelism is not a biblical word. Nor for that matter is it a Presbyterian word of long standing. The earliest creed in the *Book of Confessions* to use it is the Confession of 1967. Scripture and our tradition are not primarily concerned with a program, a set of methods, an articulation of goals and how they are to be reached—all the *ism* of evangel*ism*. They are concerned with the evangel, the gospel.

The derivation of our English word "gospel" is a matter of debate. Does it come from "good spell," a good story, or from "God spell," God's story? There is little debate, however, about the meaning of the Greek word, which gospel translates and evangel transliterates. *Evangelion* means a good message, a good announcement, good news. In secular Greek, *evangelion* was often tidings of victory in battle, or of a birth, or of a marriage. As the emperor cult developed, it was the standard word for news of auspicious events in the emperor's family.[2]

There is also a Greek verb, *evangelizein,* which usually appears in the middle voice. The transliteration "evangelize" is not a good translation. For many, evangelize carries the meaning "to convert" and usually has as its object the people to be converted.[3] *Evangelizein,* on the other hand, carries the meaning "to proclaim good news" and normally has as its object what is proclaimed. Customary English translations are circumlocutions: to bring good news, to preach good news, or simply to preach. As a result, readers of English translations can readily discern the presence of *evangelion,* but are often unaware of the presence of *evangelizein.*

We should consider also the Greek noun *evangelistes,* which easily transliterates into our English "evangelist." It clearly means "one who preaches good news." In later developments it came to mean an assistant to the apostles, a reader of the lectionary, and finally an author of one of the four New Testament books which came to be called the four Gospels.

Despite translation difficulties, what lies at the root of all three Greek words is clear enough. It has never been caught better than in the King James Version of the angel's announcement to the shepherds: "Behold, I bring you good tidings of great joy" (Luke 2:10).

THE GOSPEL IN THE NEW TESTAMENT

What are these tidings? What is the essential content of the gospel? When we turn to the New Testament, we find some interesting shifts in content and some equally interesting constants.

The Gospel according to Jesus

The first three Gospels present Jesus as a proclaimer of the gospel. Mark says that Jesus came into Galilee proclaiming the *evangelion* (1:14). Matthew describes Jesus' Galilean ministry as teaching, proclaiming the *evangelion,* and healing (4:23; 9:35). Luke, who prefers the verb *evangelizein,* speaks of Jesus' bringing the good news in Galilee (4:43; 8:1) and even in the temple at Jerusalem (20:1). What was the good news that Jesus proclaimed?

1. Jesus' evangelion *concerned the reign of God.* Mark records it this way, "The time is fulfilled, and the kingdom of God has come near; repent, and believe in the *evangelion"* (1:15). In agreement, Matthew refers to the *evangelion* as "the good news of the kingdom" (4:23; 9:35; 24:14). And in Luke, the object of the verb *evangelizein* is the kingdom of God (4:43; 8:1).

It is well known that the centerpiece of Jesus' preaching was the kingdom of God or the kingdom of heaven in Matthew's usage. Jesus compares it to various earthly realities in his parables. He describes the qualifications for entering it. He urges his followers to watch for it and to pray for its coming. In agreement with Old Testament eschatology, he says that the reign of God will include the nations, as well as Israel (Matt. 8:11; Luke 13:29).[4] The reign of God, he says, will involve a great reversal of the values of the present world. It will belong to the poor instead of to the rich (Luke 6:20, 24; Mark 10:23–27 and par.). It will belong to little children instead of to adults (Mark 10:14–15 and par.). It will belong to infants instead of to the wise and intelligent (Matt. 11:25 and par.). The last will be first and the first last (Mark 10:31 and par.). The great ones in the reign of God will be humble as a little child instead of ambitious and proud (Matt. 18:1–4). Tax collectors and prostitutes will go into the reign of God ahead of proper religious people (Matt. 21:31). Those who exalt themselves will be humbled, and those who humble themselves will be exalted (Matt. 23:12; Luke 14:11; 18:14).

Jesus' most arresting announcement is that the reign of God has already, in some sense, arrived. It has "come near" (Matt. 4:17; 10:7; Mark 1:15; Luke 10:9, 11). It has "come to you" (Matt. 12:28; Luke 11:20). It is "among you" (Luke 17:21). It is present in a hidden and dynamic way, like seed sown in the soil or yeast mixed in the dough (Matt. 13:31–33; Mark 4:26–32; Luke 13:18–21). The seed will sprout, the dough will rise. Even so, the kingdom of God is already at work in the world and will surely come in its fullness!

Jesus' *evangelion* was indeed *news,* something new, startling, undreamed of. It marked an epoch. John the Baptist, the forerunner, was the hinge of the epoch. "The law and the prophets were in effect until John came; since then the good news of the kingdom of God is proclaimed" (Luke 16:16; cf. Luke 3:18; Mark 1:1–4; Acts 10:36–37).

2. Jesus' evangelion *was embodied in himself.* Jesus not only announced the *evangelion* in his teaching and preaching, he demonstrated it; he embodied it. It is his own presence that makes the reign of God more than a future hope, that makes it a present, though hidden reality (Matt. 12:41–42; Luke 10:23; 11:31–32). His struggle with and victories over disease and death were signs of the presence of the kingdom. Especially his combat with and triumph over the unclean spirits actualized the kingdom. "If it is by the finger of God that I cast out the demons, then the kingdom of God has come to you" (Luke 11:20). What has happened, he said, is that the "strong man," the great power arrayed against God, has been overcome by "one stronger than he," namely, Jesus acting in the power of the Spirit of God (Luke 11:21–22).

3. The evangelion *of Jesus was addressed in a special way to the poor.* With its word of the great reversal it was especially good news for them. In his sermon at Nazareth, Jesus, quoting Isaiah, says:

The Spirit of the Lord is upon me,
    because he has anointed me to bring good news to the poor.
                                                    (Luke 4:18)

And in his reply to John the Baptist's question he says:

Go and tell John what you have seen and heard: the blind receive their sight, the lame walk, the lepers are cleansed, the deaf hear, the dead are raised, the poor have good news brought to them. (Luke 7:22; Matt. 11:5)

The Gospel in Apostolic Preaching

The first apostles and their helpers are presented to us as preachers of the gospel. *Evangelizein* is used of them in Acts 5:42; 8:4, 12, 25, 35, 40; 11:20. In one case, what is preached is "the kingdom of God," echoing the gospel that Jesus preached (Acts 8:12). But in others there are hints of a change of content: "Jesus as the Messiah" (Acts 5:42), "the Lord Jesus" (Acts 11:20).

A generation ago, C. H. Dodd conducted a penetrating inquiry into what this gospel was that the first apostles preached.[5] Although he concentrates on the Greek word *kērygma* (preaching) rather than on *evangelion* (good news), he explicitly states that the two are virtual equivalents.[6] But when he analyzes the sermons in Acts something quite different from the preaching of Jesus emerges. We may summarize what he finds as follows:

The age of fulfillment has dawned.
This has taken place through the ministry, death, and resurrection of Jesus, of which a brief account is given, with proof from the Scriptures that all took place through "the determinate counsel and foreknowledge of God."

By virtue of the resurrection, Jesus has been exalted at the
right hand of God, as messianic head of the new Israel.
The Holy Spirit in the Church is the sign of Christ's present
power and glory.
The Messianic Age will shortly reach its consummation in the
return of Christ.
An appeal for repentance, the offer of forgiveness and of the
Holy Spirit, and the promise of "salvation," that is, of "the life
of the Age to Come," to those who enter the elect community.[7]

We can see from this that the *evangelion of* Jesus has been
largely replaced by an *evangelion about* Jesus. This is sometimes
described in such phrases as "the proclaimer has become the proclaimed" or "the messenger has become the message." If the implication is that the gospel of Jesus has been completely distorted and
forgotten, we must demur. Remember that Jesus himself linked the
proclaimer and the proclamation, the messenger and the message.
He identified the hidden presence of the reign of God with his own
presence, saw the coming victory of God prefigured by his own victory over the unclean spirits.

Nevertheless, the intervening events between Jesus' preaching
and the preaching of the apostles—the crucifixion and the resurrection and Pentecost—did make dramatic changes in the presentation
of the gospel. The gospel that Jesus preached has been changed in
form to meet the new circumstances. The good news is not so much
the kingdom of God, with its great reversal, as it is the death and
resurrection and exaltation of Jesus. God's victory over the hostile
powers is seen, not so much in the exorcisms of Jesus as in his exaltation to the right hand of God, where his enemies are made a
stool for his feet. The sense of imminent expectation is now for the
return of Jesus and the consummation of the Messianic Age, which
has already been initiated.

The Gospel according to Paul

In the letters of Paul, *evangelion* is a frequent, important central term.[8] It is striking that Paul, using the word *evangelion* so

frequently, does not often indicate the contents of the gospel that he preached. It is most often simply "the gospel," as if he were sure that his readers already knew the contents of that term. In the case of those congregations he had founded and to which he had preached, they did know. Happily, there are two well-known passages in which Paul details briefly the high points of the *evangelion*.

In Romans 1:1–4, Paul says that the *evangelion* of God:

> was promised through the prophets in the scriptures,
> concerns God's Son,
> descended from David according to the flesh,
> declared Son of God with power according to the Spirit of holiness,
> by resurrection from the dead, Jesus Christ our Lord.

In 1 Corinthians 15:1–11, Paul reminds the Corinthians of the "gospel which he gospeled" to them (using both the verb and the noun):

> that Christ died for our sins,
> that he was buried,
> that he was raised on the third day,
> that he appeared to various believers.

The death and the resurrection, he stresses, were "in accordance with the scriptures."

In these two passages there is nothing that is not already familiar to us from our discussion of the apostolic preaching. Paul insists that this is the gospel that he had "received" (1 Cor. 15:3). "Whether then it was I or they, so we proclaim and so you have come to believe" (v. 11).

Paul knows of Jesus' gospel regarding the near approach and hidden presence of the reign of God. Luke speaks freely of Paul's preaching the kingdom (Acts 14:23; 19:8; 20:25; 28:23, 31). Paul's letters show that those who heard his preaching were familiar with the kingdom (1 Cor. 4:20; 6:9; Gal. 5:21; Col. 1:13; 4:11; 1 Thess. 2:12; 2 Thess. 1:5). But when Paul speaks of "the gospel of Christ" (Rom. 15:19; 2 Cor. 9:13; 10:14; Gal. 1:7; Phil. 1:27; 1 Thess. 3:2); "the gospel of our Lord Jesus" (2 Thess. 1:8); "the gospel of God's

Son" (Rom. 1:9); or "the gospel of God" (Rom. 1:1; 2 Cor. 11:7; 1 Thess. 2:2, 8, 9), it is not so much the good news of God's imminent and hidden reign as it is the good news of what God has done in Christ.[9] The same shift has occurred that occurred in the apostolic preaching. The point of Dodd's book is that there is an essential agreement between the *kērygma* of Paul and the *kērygma* of the sermons in Acts.

However, in Paul there are further developments. Wayne Meeks argues for another change in the *evangelion,* a change in its primary audience.[10] Jesus, touring the villages and countryside of Galilee, had good news for the poor, as we have seen. Paul, moving from city to city, attracted hearers from many levels of urban society. A study of often overlooked details in his letters reveals that the congregations founded by Paul and other missionaries, while containing few from the top levels of society and probably few from the very bottom level, contained members from a diversity of levels in the middle.

We must be cautious here. The audience was clearly enlarged, but the poor were not abandoned. Paul could still claim that his audience was "low and despised in the world," containing "not many wise, not many powerful, not many of noble birth" (1 Cor. 1:26–29).

A more striking development is that there is no longer a single *evangelion* about what God has done in Jesus. We hear of "a different gospel," which is not really "another gospel," but a perversion of the gospel (Gal. 1:6–9; 2 Cor. 11:4). This leads Paul to speak of "my gospel" (Rom. 2:16; 16:25) and "our gospel" (2 Cor. 4:3; 1 Thess. 1:5; 2 Thess. 2:14) and "the gospel that I preach" (1 Cor. 15:1; Gal. 1:11; 2:2).

To the "received" gospel Paul has added something, something that he is convinced came to him by direct revelation, something that is now an essential part of the gospel, something that to omit is to pervert the gospel. That something is the good news that the actions of God in Christ are for the benefit of the Gentiles as well as the Jews. Thus, in the Romans 1 passage, he goes on immediately to speak of his apostleship "to bring about the obedience of faith among all the Gentiles" (Rom. 1:5). This is now part of the gospel of God for which he has been "set apart" (v. 1). In Galatians 2:1–10 he speaks of being "entrusted with the gospel for the uncircumcised" (Gal. 2:7) and of receiving apostolic approval of "the gospel that I proclaim among the Gentiles" (v. 2). In the letter to the Ephesians, whether by Paul or by one of his disciples, this addition to the gospel is exalted as an eternal truth, God's hidden secret (mystery) through the ages, now revealed to his holy apostles and prophets by the Spirit, "that is, the Gentiles have become fellow heirs, members of the same body, and sharers in the promise in Christ Jesus through the *evangelion*" (Eph. 3:1–6). It is of this gospel that Paul has become the servant (*diakonos*), "to *evangelizein* to the Gentiles the news of the boundless riches of Christ." Through the church this good news will even reach "the rulers and authorities in the heavenly places" (vs. 7–11).

The inclusion of the Gentiles is not an entirely new idea with Paul. It was part of the eschatological hope of the Old Testament prophets and of Jesus. What is new is that the hope has been made present fact by the death and resurrection of Jesus. God will bring it about, but the church does not have to wait for some distant future. The church can and must help implement God's purpose for the Gentiles now!

The Constants in the
New Testament *Evangelion*

Thus far we have been examining the variables in the *evangelion*. The content of the *evangelion* can change with new events like the cross and the resurrection or with new insights like the inclusion of the Gentiles. The audience of the *evangelion* can change as missionary strategy changes. Does this make the *evangelion* a "nose of wax" that people can twist and shape to their own pleasure? If not, then what are the constants in the *evangelion?*

1. The *evangelion* is *good* news. This is true in Jesus, in the apostolic preaching, and in Paul. We have said that it is "good tidings of great joy." The following words are attributed to William Tyndale: "Evangelion (that we call the gospel) is a Greek word, and signifieth good, merry, glad and joyful tidings, that maketh a man's heart glad, and maketh him sing, dance and leap for joy."[11] The gospel is like a woman who receives a letter or a telephone call, rushes out hatless and coatless to her neighbor's house, enters without knocking or ringing, and cries in a loud voice: "The most wonderful thing has

happened!"[12] This means that the gospel is not bad news, not a pronouncement of judgment, not a diatribe of condemnation. Bad news may be at times a necessary part of life, a necessary part of scripture, a necessary part of the preaching of the church, but it is not the gospel.

2. The *evangelion* is good *news*. It is not a description of the way things have always been. Something has happened. There has been a radical, unexpected change—not just a change in me and in my feeling about things, but a change out there in the very structure and fabric of things. In Jesus, in the apostolic preaching, and in Paul there is *news:* the rule of God over a wayward world has drawn near; Jesus has been exalted to God's right hand; the Gentiles have been included. This means that the gospel is not an argument, not a theological system. There is a place for arguments and systems, but they are not the gospel.

3. The *evangelion* concerns *God's action,* not human action: what God has done, is doing, and will do in Christ, not what we must do. To be sure, the gospel must be heard, appropriated, responded to by human beings. Jesus, the apostolic preachers, and Paul all have much to say about the necessary human response. But that response is not itself part of the gospel. This means that discussions of faith and repentance, of good works and perseverance, however necessary they are and however accurate they may be in describing "the way of salvation," are not themselves part of the gospel.

4. God's action in the *evangelion* involves *struggle and victory.* In the Gospels, Jesus struggles with the unclean spirits and in conquering them makes the kingdom of God present reality. In the apostolic preaching, God raises Jesus from death, which can no longer hold him in its power; God is engaged in making Christ's enemies a stool for his feet. In Colossians, Christ "disarmed the rulers and authorities and made a public example of them, triumphing over them" in the cross (2:15).

5. The *evangelion* points beyond itself to still greater victories in the future. It is full of *hope* and *expectation.* It concerns not only what God has done and is doing but what God will do. In the teaching of Jesus, the kingdom of God is present reality, but it will come in the future in the fullness of power and glory. In the apostolic

preaching, Christ sits now at God's right hand, but he will come to judge and set things right. For Paul the future judgment is part of "my gospel" (Rom. 2:16), and for Paul's disciples "hope has been promised by the gospel" (Col. 1:23).

The New Testament picture of the gospel could be further enriched by noting the usage of *evangelion* in the Pastorals, 1 Peter, and the Apocalypse. Further light could be shed from the Johannine literature, even though it does not contain the word *evangelion*. But the essentials are before us.

As we ponder them, an enormous difficulty confronts us. How can this understanding of the gospel be sustained when centuries have passed and the hoped-for consummation of all things has not occurred? More specifically, how can the gospel be *news* when it has been heard so widely and for so long a time?

THE GOSPEL IN THE
REFORMED TRADITION

The Rise of Christendom

Following the conversion of Constantine, Christianity became more and more the "official religion" of the Roman Empire. Outside the boundaries of the empire, the gospel was still news, as missionaries carried it east and west to tribes and people who had never heard it. But within those boundaries, virtually everyone was nominally Christian. Everyone had heard the gospel, although many had doubtless only heard of it without understanding it. Rightly or wrongly it was hardly considered *news* anymore.

The Roman Empire fell, but a distinctly Christian territory survived and came to be called Christendom. Christendom expanded north and west as the tribes that brought about the empire's collapse were Christianized. Its boundaries also contracted as the Muslim conquests took over what had been initially the cradle of Christendom in the Middle East.

By the time of the Reformation, Christendom and Europe were roughly coterminous. Within Christendom/Europe it was assumed that everyone had heard the gospel and that everyone was familiar with the gospel story, even those who could not read it, since they received it through the round of the church year and the pictures in church windows. Actually biblical ignorance and superstition were widespread. Christendom was more an assumption than a fact. Many of the best minds sensed that the primitive gospel had been badly corrupted by traditions that were no part of it. But it was hard to think of the gospel as startling news.

The Gospel in Calvin

John Calvin, with his splendid grasp of scripture, understood and honored the contents of the gospel. This is quite clear in his commentaries. In "The Argument" with which he opens his commentary on the Gospels, he moves immediately to cite Romans 1:2–4 as "a clear and certain definition of the word *Gospel*." It is, he says, "a joyful message, by which God declares that he has accomplished those things which he had formerly required them to expect."

> The *Gospel,* therefore, is a public exhibition of the Son of God *manifested in the flesh* (1 Tim. iii 16) to deliver a ruined world, and to restore men from death to life. It is justly called *a good and joyful message,* for it contains perfect happiness. Its object is to commence the reign of God.[13]

Calvin understood that Jesus had preached a gospel of the kingdom of God.[14] He understood that the preaching of the gospel of the kingdom marked an epoch. He cites Luke 16:16 as evidence that the prophets were not ministers of the gospel; the gospel began with John the Baptist and Jesus.[15] He understood that for Paul the cross and resurrection of Christ stood at the heart of the gospel.[16] He even understood that the gospel had once been news. The inclusion of the Gentiles was certainly a novelty. But more than that, "the gospel was itself a novelty; for it had never till [then] been heard of, and yet was acknowledged by all the godly to have come from heaven."[17]

The question was, Could the gospel still be news, even within Christendom? Certainly the original purity and simplicity of the gospel needed to be recovered by ridding it of the accretions and corruptions of medieval Catholicism. Catholics needed to be "converted" to the Reformed faith. This was the focus of Calvin's considerable missionary zeal to make Geneva a center of missionary training and activity. But the recovery of the old is not exactly the same as the joyous announcement of the new. Calvin seems to assume that the gospel, which has been corrupted and now needs to be purified, is something that everyone has heard about and known about for a long time.

It is significant that the word "gospel" does not occur with great frequency in Calvin's most influential work, his *Institutes of the Christian Religion*.[18] His only extensive use of the word "gospel" is in his discussion of the similarities and differences between the Old and New Testaments.[19] Here he states again that the gospel was once news: "a new and unusual sort of embassy (cf. 2 Cor. 5:20) by which God has fulfilled what he had promised."[20] But the weight of the argument is that the gospel was already latent in the Old Testament; the gospel only makes patent what had already been "glimpsed in shadowed outline."[21] Calvin opposes the heresy of Marcion and wants to put the two Testaments as much on the same level as he can. So he says:

> The opposition between law and gospel ought not to be exaggerated. . . . The gospel did not so supplant the entire law as to bring forward a different way of salvation. Rather, it confirmed and satisfied whatever the law had promised, and gave substance to its shadows. . . . Where the whole law is concerned, the gospel differs from it only in clarity of manifestation.[22]

The gospel marks a new epoch, but the weight of Calvin's argument in the *Institutes* is that the new epoch was not all that new after all. The quality of the gospel as news is severely attenuated.

The Gospel in Reformed Confessions

It should not surprise us, then, that when the followers of Calvin came to write creeds and confessions, the word "gospel" was not prominent in them.[23]

The writers of the Scots Confession (1560) declared in their preface:

> With all humility we embrace the purity of Christ's gospel, which is the only food of our souls, and therefore so precious to us, that we are determined to suffer the extremest of worldly danger, rather than suffer ourselves to be defrauded of the same.[24]

The context would seem to indicate that "Christ's gospel" serves here as a synonym for the holy scriptures as a whole, rather than a designation for Christ's preaching of the kingdom. The body of the confession mentions ministers of the gospel as the only lawful administrators of the sacraments, but what the gospel is is not defined or discussed.[25]

The Heidelberg Catechism (1563) states that the Holy Spirit creates faith in our hearts "by the preaching of the holy gospel,"[26] and that "the preaching of the holy gospel" opens and shuts the kingdom of heaven.[27] But the only discussion of what the gospel is is the statement that a summary of the gospel is taught in the articles of the Apostles' Creed.[28]

The Second Helvetic Confession (1566) stands alone in devoting an entire chapter to the gospels, titled "Of the Gospel of Jesus Christ, of the Promises, and of the Spirit and Letter."[29] It begins in good Calvinistic fashion by seeking to reduce the difference between the two Testaments. It even goes beyond Calvin in finding the gospel in the Old Testament. "It is most certain that those who were before the law and under the law were not altogether destitute of the Gospel. For they had extraordinary evangelical promises."[30] Properly speaking, however, the gospel is

> glad and joyous news, in which, first by John the Baptist, then by Christ the Lord himself, and afterwards by the apostles and their successors, is preached to us in the world that God has now performed what he promised from the beginning of the world, and has sent, nay more, has given us his only Son and in him reconciliation with the Father, the remission of sins, all fulness and everlasting life.[31]

Just as the Scots Confession broadens the meaning of gospel to include all the scriptures, and the Heidelberg Catechism to include all the doctrines of the Apostles' Creed, so the Second Helvetic Confession proceeds to broaden "the gospel properly speaking" to include the entire New Testament:

Therefore, the history delineated by the four Evangelists and explaining how these things were done or fulfilled by Christ, what things Christ taught and did, and that those who believe in him have all fulness, is rightly called the Gospel. The preaching and writings of the apostles, in which the apostles explain for us how the Son was given to us by the Father, and in him everything that has to do with life and salvation, is also rightly called evangelical doctrine, so that not even today, if sincerely preached, does it lose its illustrious title.[32]

The more broadly the gospel is defined, the more it loses its character as news and becomes, instead, "evangelical doctrine." Indeed, the Second Helvetic Confession ends its discussion by declaring that the gospel "seemed to be a new doctrine when first preached by Christ . . . , yet actually it not only was and still is an old doctrine . . . , but is the most ancient of all in the world."[33]

The word "gospel" appears with some frequency in the Westminster Confession of Faith (1647). The two epochs of the law and the gospel are often mentioned.[34] One of the marks of the church is that "the doctrine of the gospel is taught and embraced."[35] A part of the power of the keys is to open the kingdom of heaven to the penitent "by the ministry of the gospel."[36] Church censures are necessary for vindicating "the holy profession of the gospel."[37] The wicked "obey not the gospel of Jesus Christ."[38] Despite these several occurrences of the word, we have moved further than ever from the gospel as good news. It is the name of a historical epoch; it is doctrine to be taught, discipline to be exercised, rules to be obeyed.

The Westminster Confession of Faith is primarily interested in the effects of the gospel on the individual human heart. The core of the confession is a penetrating analysis of the *ordo salutis* (the way of salvation). Because of Westminster's profound influence on American Presbyterianism, evangelism has often been understood by Presbyterians as leading unbelievers through the steps of saving faith, repentance unto life, good works, perseverance, and assurance. When the persons being evangelized can demonstrate an understanding of the difference between justification by works and justification by faith, when they can distinguish between justification and adoption on one hand and sanctification on the other, then evangelism has succeeded. These are all matters of great importance and need at some point to be understood. But they are not the evangel. The evangel, as we have seen, is good news about God's action; a careful understanding of our actions in response is another matter.

THE AMERICAN EXPERIMENT

The transplantation of Reformed Christianity to North America had profound effects on its understanding of the gospel. It was not just a geographical move, but a move from parishes, where the church had access to everyone, to a more loosely organized society where there were many to whom the church had no access. How was the gospel to be communicated to them?

Also there was constant contact between Christians and the Native Americans, who were clearly outside of Christendom, people for whom the gospel was news indeed. The struggles of men like John Eliot and David Brainerd to communicate the gospel to the Native Americans raised afresh the question of what the gospel is.

The Great Awakening

An event that left a permanent stamp on evangelism in North America was the Great Awakening of the 1740s. As one reads representative documents of the period, one is struck yet again with the paucity of references to the gospel. That "a great work of God" occurred there is no doubt. That there were many sincere and far-reaching conversions is an unassailable fact. That the course of our national history was altered by it is a judgment that commands wide assent. But what part did the good news play in all of this?

It is manifestly unfair to see the Great Awakening as totally dominated by bad news. The sermon "Sinners in the Hand of an Angry God" is typical neither of Jonathan Edwards nor of the Awakening as a whole. George Whitefield, whose preaching played a decisive role in inaugurating the Awakening, says in a characteristic sermon:

> If you will not be drawn by the Cords of Infinite and everlasting Love, what will draw you? I could urge many terrors of the Lord to persuade you; but if the Love of *Jesus Christ* will not constrain you, your Case is desperate.[39]

17

This being said, it is also true that "preaching the terrors of the law" was widespread during the Awakening. Presbyterian revivalists like Gilbert Tennent commonly emphasized the contrast between divine righteousness as found in the scriptural law and the meager good works of their hearers in order to show them their damnable state before God and to prompt them to become Christians.[40] In this way, proclaiming bad news before the good news of the gospel became for many Americans the normal sequence of evangelistic preaching even to the present day.

What the Congregationalists in New England and the Presbyterians in the Middle Colonies mainly preached during the First Great Awakening was basic Calvinistic doctrines, right out of the Westminster Confession of Faith: original sin, the imputation of Christ's righteousness, justification by faith alone, faith as the gift of God. In those places and at that time, such preaching was a powerful engine of conversion and awakening. It established another benchmark for American evangelism.

Was there any *news* in all this? The unprecedented results of this preaching—the vast crowds, the tears, the crying out, the physical contortions of some of the hearers—bestowed an aura of news on doctrines that had long been familiar. Certainly the results made the preaching newsworthy; the newspapers were full of accounts of sermons.

Beyond that, there was in certain quarters a return to news that had not been sounded in the Reformed confessions: the gospel note that the kingdom of God had drawn near. Jonathan Edwards saw the Awakening as the opening act of further works of God that would usher in the time of the kingdom of heaven on earth: a time of great light and knowledge, a time of greater holiness, a time of great peace and love, a time of excellent order in the church. This would come on swiftly, yet gradually. It would not be a project of human effort, any more than the Awakening had been; it would be God's project.[41]

Aaron Burr (senior), Edwards's son-in-law, foresaw the overthrow of the Church of Rome, the end of the Turkish Empire, the increase of the world's population, the universal promotion of true Christianity, the end of war, powerful preaching of the gospel, and multiplied conversions, particularly among the Jews. He expected all this to come quickly.[42] Here we see the millenarian note that was to mark much subsequent American evangelism.

The Missionary Movement

In one of his brilliant generalizations, H. Richard Niebuhr saw the seventeenth century in America as devoted to the reign of God, God's sovereignty in all things; the eighteenth century as devoted to the rule of Christ in the hearts of believers; and the nineteenth century as devoted to the coming kingdom of God on earth.[43] With the nineteenth century, evangelism moved beyond words to include action. The revivalist Charles G. Finney, for example, believed that persons who were converted to God and God's interests would inevitably bring forth fruits of righteousness affecting human society. "The cause of peace, the cause of antislavery, and that of the overthrow of licentiousness must lie near the heart of every truly benevolent mind."[44]

Of all the causes that blossomed as a result of the First and Second Great Awakenings, the one that spoke most often of the gospel was the missionary movement. Here the gospel was once again news, news announced to peoples and nations that had never heard it before. Much of the extraordinary dynamic of the missionary movement derived from that fact. It will suffice to quote some of the familiar missionary hymns:

> We've a story to tell to the nations,
>   That shall turn their hearts to the right,
> A story of truth and mercy,
>   A story of peace and light.
> For the darkness shall turn to dawning,
>   And the dawning to noonday bright,
> And Christ's great Kingdom shall come on earth,
>   The Kingdom of love and light. (1896)

> Publish glad tidings, tidings of peace,
> Tidings of Jesus, redemption and release. (1870)

> Heralds of Christ, who bear the King's commands,
> Immortal tidings in your mortal hands,
> Pass on and carry swift the news ye bring,
> Make straight, make straight the highway of the King. (1894)

It is amazing to see how the New Testament *evangelion,* and *especially the gospel* as proclaimed by Jesus, suddenly reappears after centuries of eclipse.

Even the sacrosanct Westminster Confession of Faith could not withstand the renewed enthusiasm for the gospel that marked the missionary movement. In 1903 the Presbyterian Church in the United States of America added Chapter XXXV, "Of the Gospel of the Love of God and Missions." The Presbyterian Church in the United States followed suit, adding the same text, but as Chapter X, titled simply "Of the Gospel." The chapter is clearly intended as an antidote for Chapter III, "Of God's Eternal Decrees," which seemed at that time to cut the nerve of evangelistic efforts and foreign missions with its declaration that the number of human beings and angels who are predestinated to everlasting life and the number foreordained to everlasting death "is so certain and definite that it cannot be either increased or diminished."[45] The word "gospel" resounds throughout the new chapter, but it lacks the note of *news* that was so prominent in the missionary hymns. It refers mainly to the general graciousness of God.

Despite its startling recovery of the *news* of the gospel, the missionary movement did not represent a complete return to the New Testament understanding of the evangel. The notion of Christendom was alive and well. Now including North America as well as Europe, Christendom was the base from which the missionaries went forth to heathendom. It was not clear whether the gospel was news within Christendom or only beyond it. Nor was the major notice for missions the goodness of the good news. It was pity for the perishing. One remembers the speakers at the great Student Volunteer Movement conventions, standing on the platform, watches in hand, counting the souls that were falling into hell second by second because no one had told them the news.

THE PRESENT SITUATION

Institutionalization and secularization are marks of the present century.[46] Institutions are necessary efforts to preserve the gains of previous movements and enthusiasms. For example, the great century of missionary enthusiasm is commonly conceded to have ended around 1914, but the gains have been institutionalized in church mission boards and parachurch missions. Important work continues, but mention of the gospel has greatly diminished.

The institutionalization of evangelism was eloquently described by H. Richard Niebuhr as early as 1937. The ways of entering the kingdom of Christ, he says, are

> defined, mapped, motorized and equipped with guard rails.
>
> Regeneration, the dying to the old self and the rising to new life . . . becomes conversion which takes place on Sunday morning during the singing of the last hymn or twice a year when the revival preacher comes to town. . . . It is not so much the road from the temporal to the eternal, from trust in the finite to faith in the infinite, from self-centeredness to God-centeredness, as it is the way into the institutionalized church or the company of respectable Christian churchmen.[47]

One can only wonder how Niebuhr would have described the subsequent development of TV evangelistic ministries or the employment of marketing experts by today's megachurches.

In the current scene is there any way to bring the evangel back into evangelism? In our brief study of the New Testament we defined the *evangelion* as good news, not bad news; as news, not argument or theological system; as the work of God, not the manipulation of human beings; as struggle and victory over the unruly powers; as hope and expectation for the future. From our rapid survey of Presbyterian history it is clear that "gospel" has been used as the name of an epoch, a synonym for the whole Bible, or the New Testament, or the Apostles' Creed. Chiefly in the missionary movement was there a partial recapture of its original meaning. Can we hope for a more complete recapture as our century moves toward its close?

In the providence of God there are some developments that may favor a recapture of the *evangelion*. One is the final collapse of Christendom. In the great century of missionary enthusiasm, Christendom survived as the home base from which the missionaries went forth to the lands beyond Christendom's bounds. Today one cannot draw a map of Christendom. Indigenous churches are found in almost every nation, often experiencing more rapid growth than the former "sending" churches. Old Christendom has become a mission field. There's a Buddhist on the block, a mosque near the mall. And there are millions without any religion and millions more with a nominal Christianity that is largely unrelated to the gospel. The persistent problem, noted throughout this survey, is: How can the gospel be news when everybody has heard it many times? But everyone in America today has not heard it. There is news to be published!

Another development is the rise of Reformed theologies that are more hospitable to the good news of the *evangelion*. Karl Barth has been called God's joyful partisan. His recasting of the Reformed doctrine of election is not, as has often been asserted, a turn to universalism, but it is good news of an extraordinary kind.[48] Barth goes on to say that what makes a Christian a Christian is not good works, or the reception of grace, but the call to be a witness to the good news of God's grace to all in the world, even those who will not accept it.[49] Jürgen Moltmann in his "theology of hope" draws together *epangelia* (promise) and *evangelion* (gospel) in a way that stresses good news.[50] Recent Presbyterian creeds use the word "gospel" in its New Testament sense.[51] If the Presbyterian Church should ever become interested again in theology, it would find solid theological grounds for an evangelism that embraces the evangel.

Another development is the increase of cross-cultural experiences. The globe is shrinking; the global village is more and more of a reality. Missionaries come from the younger churches to the churches of what used to be Christendom. We have the opportunity, if we are humble enough, to be hearers of the gospel as well as proclaimers. That is most important, for it is only as we hear the gospel as news for ourselves that we are able to proclaim it as news for others.

Let me illustrate from a personal experience. One Saturday, in Accra, Ghana, where I was attending a meeting of the Faith and Order Commission of the World Council of Churches, I witnessed a fascinating ceremony. A number of tribal chiefs came in from the countryside, twirling their umbrellas, the symbols of their power. Members of their tribes who had moved to the city gathered around them in adoration and celebration. The next day, Sunday, I was seated in the Roman Catholic Cathedral of Accra, waiting for worship to begin, enjoying the carvings of various African animals that formed the altar rail. Over the altar hung a conventional, European crucifix. But what was that above the crucifix? I finally made it out—a chief's umbrella! That bleeding, broken man on the cross is the chief! Suddenly that polished relic, that cherished antique, that oldest of Christian confessions, "Jesus is Lord," was new. It was news! I felt an irrepressible urge to proclaim the news to anyone who would listen.

What is lacking in Presbyterian evangelism is not a theoretical priority; the church has declared that many times. It is not methods and materials. It is motivation. Pity for those perishing without Christ, which was a key to the old missionary enthusiasm, does not seem to work anymore. Nor do guilt and shame. Institutional alarm over declining membership has led to competitive blame-placing more than to evangelism. If we could see the gospel once again as good news, it would be its own motivation. Good news, by its very nature, has to be shared. It "maketh a man's heart glad, and maketh him sing, dance and leap for joy." It sends a woman hatless and coatless to her neighbor's house: "The most wonderful thing has happened!"

The gospel is indeed old news, familiar news, heard before. But that does not keep it from being new news, startling, unexpected, bordering on the absurd. And it is above all good news. The Presbyterian novelist-preacher Frederick Buechner says that the gospel is too good to be true. But beyond that, it is too good not to be true.[52]

NOTES

1. Peter Stuhlmacher, professor of New Testament at Tübingen, has said that every day of his life and scholarship is energized by asking again and again the same question, "What is the gospel?"

2. For a full discussion of *evangelion,* see Gerhard Friedrich's article in *Theological Dictionary of the New Testament,* ed. Gerhard Kittel and Gerhard Friedrich, trans. Geoffrey W. Bromiley (Grand Rapids: Wm. B. Eerdmans Publishing Co., 1964–1976), 2:707–37.

3. This is not to say that conversion is an unimportant topic in the consideration of the Presbyterian evangelistic heritage or that the proclamation and hearing of the gospel are not crucial to conversion.

4. Donald E. Gowan, "How Christianity Became an Evangelistic Religion: Old Testament Evidence," and Virgil Cruz, "How Christianity Became an Evangelistic Religion: A Survey of Some Pertinent New Testament Material" (papers presented at the Faithful Witness Conference, Louisville Presbyterian Theological Seminary, Louisville, Ky., March 18–19, 1993).

5. C. H. Dodd, *The Apostolic Preaching and Its Developments* (Edinburgh: T. & T. Clark, 1936).

6. Ibid., 8.

7. Ibid., 21–23.

8. The word *evangelion* occurs in all the letters of the accepted Pauline corpus, plus Colossians and Ephesians, plus all the Pastorals except Titus.

9. Contra the position of Gerhard Friedrich in the *Theological Dictionary of the New Testament,* 2:730–31. Friedrich argues, unconvincingly to me, that the genitives "of Christ," "of the Lord Jesus" are both subjective and objective and that Paul's "gospel" is essentially identical with what Jesus preached.

10. See Wayne Meeks, *The First Urban Christians: The Social World of the Apostle Paul* (New Haven, Conn.: Yale University Press, 1983).

11. William Tyndale, "A Pathway into the Holy Scripture," in *The Work of William Tyndale,* ed. G. E. Duffield (Philadelphia: Fortress Press, 1965), 4.

12. John Baillie gave this description of the gospel in an unpublished lecture on Mark 1:14–15 at Princeton Theological Seminary in 1947.

13. John Calvin, *Commentary on a Harmony of the Evangelists, Matthew, Mark, and Luke,* trans. William Pringle (Grand Rapids: Wm. B. Eerdmans Publishing Co., 1949) 1:xxxv–xxxvi.

14. Ibid., 224–25.

15. Ibid., xxxvii.

16. John Calvin, *Commentaries on the Epistle of Paul to the Romans,* trans. and ed. John Owen (Grand Rapids: William B. Eerdmans Publishing Co., 1947), 43–46; and John Calvin, *Commentary on the Epistles of Paul to the Corinthians,* trans. John Pringle (Grand Rapids: William B. Eerdmans Publishing Co., 1948), 2:9–13.

17. John Calvin, *Commentaries on the Epistles of Paul to the Galatians and Ephesians,* trans. William Pringle (Grand Rapids: William B. Eerdmans Publishing Co., 1948), 251.

18. *Calvin: Institutes of the Christian Religion,* ed. John T. McNeill, trans. Ford Lewis Battles The Library of Christian Classics, vols. 20 and 21 (Philadelphia: Westminster Press, 1960). Citations are given by book, chapter, and section, rather than by page number, so they can be found in any edition.

19. *Institutes,* 2.9.

20. *Institutes,* 2.9.2.

21. *Institutes,* 2.9.1.

22. *Institutes,* 2.9.4.

23. The confessions here cited may all be found in *The Constitution of*

the Presbyterian Church (U.S.A.), Part I: *Book of Confessions*, (Louisville, Ky.: Office of the General Assembly, 1991).

24. "The Scotch Confession of Faith," in *The Creeds of Christendom*, ed. Philip Schaff, 3 vols. (1877; New York: Harper & Brothers, 1919), 3:439. The language of this creed as found in this source has been modernized in spelling.

25. *Book of Confessions*, 3.22.

26. *Book of Confessions*, 4.065.

27. Ibid.

28. *Book of Confessions*, 4.022.

29. *Book of Confessions*, 5.086–.092.

30. *Book of Confessions*, 5.086.

31. *Book of Confessions*, 5.089.

32. Ibid.

33. *Book of Confessions*, 5.092.

34. *Book of Confessions*, 6.041, 6.042, 6.107, 6.117, 6.141, 6.152.

35. *Book of Confessions*, 6.143.

36. *Book of Confessions*, 6.170.

37. *Book of Confessions*, 6.171.

38. *Book of Confessions*, 6.181.

39. "The Marriage of Cana," in *The Great Awakening: Documents on the Revival of Religion, 1740–1745*, ed. Richard L. Bushman (New York: Atheneum Publishers, 1970), 33–35.

40. Gilbert Tennent, *A Solemn Warning to the Secure World, from the God of Terrible Majesty; Or, the Presumptuous Sinner Detected, his Pleas Consider'd, and his Doom Display'd* (Boston: S. Kneeland & T. Green, 1735), 70–71.

41. See Jonathan Edwards, *A History of the Work of Redemption*, in *The Great Awakening: Documents Illustrating the Crisis and Its Consequences*, ed. Alan Heimert and Perry Miller (Indianapolis: Bobbs-Merrill Co., 1967), 20–34. Published in 1777, *A History* contained sermons that were actually preached in 1739.

42. See "The Watchman's Answer," in *The Great Awakening*, 169–172.

43. H. Richard Niebuhr, *The Kingdom of God in America* (Chicago: Willett, Clark & Co., 1937).

44. Ibid., 196.

45. *Book of Confessions*, 6.016–.017.

46. Milton J Coalter, John M. Mulder, and Louis B. Weeks, *The Re-Forming Tradition: Presbyterians and Mainstream Protestantism* (Louisville, Ky.: Westminster/John Knox Press, 1992); Lesslie Newbigin, *Foolishness to the Greeks: The Gospel and Western Culture* (Grand Rapids: Wm. B. Eerdmans Publishing Co., 1986); and Robert Wuthnow, *The Struggle for America's Soul: Evangelicals, Liberals, and Secularism* (Grand Rapids: Wm. B. Eerdmans Publishing Co., 1989).

47. H. Richard Niebuhr, *The Kingdom of God in America*, 179–180.

48. Karl Barth, *Church Dogmatics,* ed. G. W. Bromiley and T. F. Torrance (Edinburgh: T. & T. Clark, 1957), II/2, 3–506.

49. Barth, *Church Dogmatics,* IV/3 (1962), 554–614.

50. Jürgen Moltmann, *Theology of Hope: On the Ground and the Implications of a Christian Eschatology,* trans. James W. Leitch (New York: Harper & Row, 1975), 139–48. Also Moltmann's *The Church in the Power of the Spirit: A Contribution to Messianic Ecclesiology,* trans. Margaret Kohl (New York: Harper & Row, 1977), 76–85.

51. The Confession of 1967, *Book of Confessions,* 9.04, 9.06, 9.20, 9.21, and A Brief Statement of Faith, *Book of Confessions,* 10.2.

52. Frederick Buechner, *Telling the Truth: The Gospel as Tragedy, Comedy, and Fairy Tale* (New York: Harper & Row, 1977), 71, 98.

2. What Is Conversion?

DAWN DeVRIES

For we are what he has made us, created in Christ Jesus for good works, which God prepared beforehand to be our way of life.

Ephesians 2:10

Thus in its origin and basis, at the superior place where it is set in motion, the conversion of man is a decision of God for him which not only makes possible a corresponding decision of man for God, the free act of his obedience, but makes this act and obedience real, directly causing it to take place.

Karl Barth, *Church Dogmatics*

To speak about conversion in the context of a book exploring the Reformed evangelistic heritage raises a peculiar set of questions. Simply addressing the question of conversion in the theological section of this book perhaps suggests a particular understanding of the goals of evangelism—-one that may or may not be agreeable to many Reformed Christians. But deeper problems arise when one reflects on the meaning of conversion as expressed in the classic texts of Reformed theology, for there one encounters a deliberate reticence. For example, it would be difficult to cull a definition of conversion from any of the eleven creeds, confessions, and catechisms in the *Book of Confessions* of the Presbyterian Church (U.S.A.).[1] This reticence about conversion in Reformed theology is neither accidental nor unimportant, but is symptomatic of some deep and lasting assumptions within the tradition about the way in which we experience the grace of Christ.

Is a Reformed theology of conversion for the twenty-first century a contradiction in terms? In order to answer this question, we

27

need first a clear understanding of what is meant by "conversion" and what the Reformed tradition has had to say about it, directly or indirectly. Further, thinking about the theology of conversion as a new century approaches raises questions specific to our historical context, and these need to be addressed before finally sketching the outlines of a contemporary Reformed theology of conversion.

CONVERSION DEFINED

For all the talk about conversion in the contemporary world, there is a surprising lack of clarity about what is meant by the term. This conceptual fuzziness extends to academic discussions of conversion as well.[2] Viewed from the perspectives of the various academic disciplines, conversion may refer to a psychological crisis, a socialization process, a cultural transformation, an act of God, or an act of human resolve. Under certain circumstances, it may be useful to have a broad enough definition to include all of these perspectives on conversion.[3] But for the purposes of this chapter, it will be more useful to limit our definition to a strictly *theological* one. Even that limitation does not solve all the problems of conceptual clarity, for different theologies of conversion will issue in different definitions. We may, however, be able to arrive at a common understanding if we examine, first of all, the sources in scripture and tradition for the concept of conversion.

The actual word "conversion" appears only once in the English Bible, in Acts 15:3. There are, however, related words that express the concept of conversion—a "turning around." In the Hebrew scriptures the most common are the various forms of *shub* (lit., a turning from and to, or a return), while in the New Testament it is *metanoia* (lit., a change of mind, or repentance).

Although scholarly discussion on the meaning of these words is complex,[4] several inferences can be drawn out from the biblical texts that use these terms in order to arrive at a theological definition of conversion.

First, the initiative in conversion is divine. The call to turn from evil and return to the good comes from God. In the Hebrew scriptures this is clear, because the turning happens in the context of the covenant. Yahweh called the people of Israel into existence in forming the Mosaic-Sinai covenant.[5] Repeatedly, Israel turns away from Yahweh in faithlessness, and Yahweh calls them to return. The call to repentance may be uttered by Moses, or Nathan, or Isaiah, but they are Yahweh's instruments: they bring the word of the Lord. This pattern of turning away and returning to God well summarizes the religious experience of Israel as a whole.

In the New Testament, it is Jesus and his disciples who voice the call to repent. But once again the initiative in the process is God's. It is because of God's concern for the world that God calls men and women to turn around, and not because they are seeking a new way of life.

Second, the biblical concept of conversion entails a series of turning points or a process rather than a single moment. In the Hebrew Scriptures, the people of Israel are called to repent and return to the Lord over and over again. While there are moments in which the conviction of sin or the call to repent come powerfully and with great clarity, they are never sufficient to last a lifetime, either for an individual or for a people.[6] Conversion must be repeated as often as the people turn away from their covenantal obligations.

In the New Testament, the need for a series of conversions, rather than a single moment of conversion, stems from the insistence that faithfulness to God's call implies a radical change both in one's personal values and behavior and also in the structures of society. Since no one can achieve these reorientations once for all, "conversion," if one uses the singular, must be a constant process made up of many moments.[7]

Third, while never discounting the need for individuals to reform their own lives, the biblical concept of conversion is linked always to a vision of the just society. Conversion is not the means by which individuals gain their own personal reward of life after death or escape from God's wrath. Rather, conversion is the vehicle for turning individuals previously preoccupied with their own desires toward God and their neighbors. In the eighth-century prophets, for example, the call to conversion is itself collective: it is issued to the people as a whole rather than to individuals. Moreover, the faithfulness that it calls for involves not merely ritual observance but, more important, attention to just relations in society. Similarly, Jesus' call to conversion as presented in the Sermon on the Mount calls for a reorienting of social values that is full of political and economic consequences.[8] In sum, the Bible does not support a view of conversion that is narrowly focused on the individual and his or her spiritual development.

But if the biblical view of conversion is not individualistic and inwardly oriented, neither, finally, is it content to rest with the transformation of values in the human community. For the most encompassing view of conversion in the Bible is *cosmic:* "In Christ God was reconciling the *world* to himself" (2 Cor. 5:19, italics added). The human community are ambassadors entrusted with the word of reconciliation, but ultimately the conversion to be achieved reaches far beyond human lives to the very cosmos.[9]

An important source for the theological definition of conversion is the stories of the conversions of significant individuals in the Christian community. The apostle Paul is the example par excellence: his story is presented by the author of Luke-Acts as the model for subsequent conversions in the church. But after Paul we can name many other exemplary conversions or rebirths, such as those of Constantine, Augustine, and Luther. These stories bring additional elements to the definition of the term, some of which are coherent, and some of which are in conflict, with the biblical view outlined above.[10] The stories present conversion as a sudden experience: something that comes "out of the blue." In many of the earliest conversion stories, ecstatic experiences accompany the moment of truth. The person sees visions or hears voices that address him or her personally. The conversion experience is presented as the dividing line between two times in the person's life. In this sense, it is decisive and once and for all. Also, the experience is often represented in the conversion stories as a change from one religion to another or from irreligion to religion, rather than as the deepening of a religious commitment already held. The emphasis is not so much on returning to the God with whom one is already involved as on first *discovering* the true God and the true way of life. Clearly, some different emphases are sounded in these conversion stories than in the biblical material presented above. In particular, they tend to highlight the suddenness and decisiveness of conversion as an individual experience.

A final source for the theological definition of conversion is precisely the various theologies of conversion in the history of Christian thought. Strangely, full-blown theologies of conversion are a relatively modern phenomenon.[11] Among the Reformed, it was the English Puritans who first distinguished themselves from what they regarded as an incomplete reformation of the church imposed by Queen Elizabeth by insisting that every believer have a conversion experience. What issued from the Puritan emphasis on conversion was not so much a theology of conversion as a series of stylized conversion narratives that were influential in forming the theological attitudes of the group.[12] These narratives followed a predictable pattern, tracing the converted person's progress from indifference to conviction of personal sin before the biblical law, followed by conversion, new being, and the transformation of self and society.

The conversion itself was understood in the context of covenant; it was regarded as the faithful human response to God's call. But, as Jerald C. Brauer notes, "English Puritans tended to isolate the doctrine of conversion from the traditional Reformation concept of justification-regeneration. . . . Their stress on the personal appropriation of salvation tended to outweigh the classical Reformation's emphasis on the givenness, the objectivity of God's action in salvation."[13]

When Puritanism passed into revivalism during the First and Second Great Awakenings in America, Brauer argues, the concept of conversion was taken even further away from the classical Reformation teaching on salvation. Conversion became more directly linked to the individual and his or her fate rather than with the elect community, and it was taken to be the determinant of all other aspects of the Christian life.[14] In addition, the steps to and the marks of true conversion began to be spelled out in ever greater detail.[15] The theology of revivalism developed the concept of conversion more fully in the eighteenth and nineteenth centuries.

In the twentieth century there has been something of a renaissance of theological interest in conversion among Roman Catholic theologians developing the work of Bernard Lonergan. While traditional Roman Catholic theologies of conversion viewed the experience as primarily a religious event with ethical implications, Lonergan argued that conversion should not be considered to be exclusively religious. Rather, conversion can be one of four kinds—religious, moral, intellectual, and psychic—-and each of them, while sharing some features, also differ from one another in significant ways.[16] This broadening of the concept can make use of much of the literature on the subject generated by the social sciences.

Is it possible, then, to arrive at a theological definition of conversion, drawn from the sources outlined above? Let us venture a definition that may embrace several of the themes already noted. *Conversion is the transformation of a person or community that arises from the discovery or deepening of beliefs about God, self, and world.*

Several things should be noted about this definition. First, it leaves open the question of where the impulse for conversion comes from: God or human searching. Although the Reformed tradition leans distinctly toward the divine in answer to this question, other theological traditions have emphasized the human search. Consequently, it seems best in a general definition to leave the matter open. Second, the definition embraces both the individual and the communal senses of conversion. Certain traditions stress one more than another, but a general definition requires both. Third, this definition is inclusive of two timetables for conversion, one more gradual and one more sudden and decisive. Finally, it notes the cognitive element (i.e., the source in belief) without denying the psychological, moral, social, and perhaps even ontological aspects of conversion.

CONVERSION IN THE
REFORMED TRADITION

Calvin's discussion of conversion occurs in Book 3 of his *Institutes of the Christian Religion.* The word "conversion" is not, however, the one Calvin favors.[17] Rather, he states, the whole "sum of the gospel is held to consist in repentance and forgiveness of sins," and it is these two gifts of union with Christ, regeneration (repentance) and justification (forgiveness), that frame his soteriology.[18]

Conversion, for Calvin, is roughly equivalent to repentance. He defines it as "the true turning of our life to God, a turning that arises from a pure and earnest fear of him; and it consists in the mortification of our flesh and of the old man, and in the vivification of the Spirit."[19]

As in so many of Calvin's dogmatic definitions, his understanding of repentance attempts to steer the middle course between two extremes: the Anabaptist and the Roman Catholic views on this doctrine. Against the Anabaptists, Calvin insists that repentance is a continual process since all Christians remain a mixture of sinfulness and righteousness.[20] But this does not mean that the Roman system of confession and satisfaction is an appropriate way of continuing the process of repentance.

Calvin devotes two long chapters to refuting the Roman doctrine of regeneration, and his arguments are complex. But the heart of the problem with Roman Catholic views of repentance, as he puts it, is this:

> They are wonderfully silent concerning the inward renewal of the mind, which bears with it true correction of life. Among them there is, indeed, much talk concerning contrition and attrition. They torture souls with many misgivings, and immerse them in a sea of trouble and anxiety. But where they seem to have wounded hearts deeply, they heal all the bitterness with a light sprinkling of ceremonies.[21]

What Calvin seeks to develop is a doctrine of regeneration that demands serious effort at moral reform and yet recognizes that repentance is a gift from God. The goal of repentance is to restore in us the image of God. This, Calvin tells us, "does not take place in one moment or one day or one year; but through continual and sometimes even slow advances."[22] It is truly God's work in us that produces the transformation, for, Calvin argues, "it would be easier for us to create men than for us of our own power to put on a more excellent nature."[23] Thus Christians seeking through following Christ to deny themselves and bear the cross can always rest confident in the assurance that God will complete in them the work of conversion that God has begun.

The most distinctive elements in Calvin's discussion of conversion, then, are its *gradual completion* and its *character as a gift*. The gift is given by God's showing himself in Jesus Christ to be worthy of trust: in short, repentance or conversion is the effect of faith in the fatherly goodwill of God revealed in the gospel.[24] While these points were directed against Calvin's theological adversaries, he believed he had discovered them through a faithful interpretation of scripture.[25]

The Second Helvetic Confession, written by the Zurich reformer Heinrich Bullinger and published by the Reformed churches of Switzerland and the Palatinate (1566), agrees closely with Calvin's treatment of conversion. Once again conversion is taken to be the functional equivalent of repentance—"a sincere turning to God and all good, and earnest turning away from the devil and all evil."[26]

Like Calvin, Bullinger develops the doctrine between the extremes of the Roman system of confession and satisfaction and any view of human perfectibility. He identifies advocates of the latter view not as Anabaptists but as "old and new Novatians and Catharists." "Repentance is a sheer gift of God and not a work of our strength." It must be exercised constantly if Christians are not to fall back into the state of sinfulness from which they have been, as it were, resurrected.[27] For Bullinger, too, conversion is a gradual process and a gratuitous gift.

By 1646 a different framework for the discussion of conversion appears in the Westminster Confession of Faith. The debate over the teaching of Arminius and the Remonstrants concerning human free will had so exercised the Reformed churches in the Netherlands several decades earlier that now it was seen as the primary problematic for a Reformed theology of grace. The debate centered around the questions: Is grace an unconditional gift of an electing God to totally depraved sinners and, therefore, both irresistible and permanent? Or, is grace the gift of God to humans whose will responds appropriately to the offer of salvation in Christ?

The Puritans who worked on the Westminster Confession and catechisms were fascinated with the subjective operations of grace. Consequently, they produced in these Westminster Standards an explosion of vocabulary and a much more careful definition of the terms than we find either in Calvin or in Bullinger.

Conversion is once again not the favored term, but now the "effectual call" and "regeneration" (as the moment of rebirth) rather than lifelong "repentance" carry the theological content of conversion. While the Westminster divines wanted above all to insist upon the prevenience of grace (i.e., that grace comes before any human response of faith), they also intensified the tension, present in smaller measure already in Calvin and Bullinger, between divine gift and human work in conversion. God draws the elect to Jesus Christ, "yet so as they come most freely, being made willing by his grace."[28] Similarly, though repentance is not the cause of pardon, it is "of such necessity to all sinners, that none may expect pardon without it."[29] Thus, although the Westminster Confession carries forward Calvin's and Bullinger's emphasis on conversion as gift and process, it changes the quality of both terms. The gift of conversion is now defined quite carefully as something for the elect that becomes operative in a moment through the effectual calling of God. Moreover, conversion only initiates a process (sanctification), which, though a work of God, is now seen to admit of gradual, measurable progress to which believers must actively be attentive.

Later Reformed theology attempted to sort out the complicated terminology of salvation. What are the relationships, it asked, between regeneration, repentance, conversion, faith, and calling? One might find several different answers to this question in various Reformed dogmatics of the eighteenth through the twentieth centuries.[30] But however the terms were sorted out, one can find in later Reformed theology the already familiar themes of conversion as gift and process.

Reformed theology has also emphasized an ecclesial or church context for conversion. Reformed theologians have insisted that conversion is a work of God through the mediation of the Word and that Word, both in preaching and sacraments, is available ordinarily in the church.[31] Thus, the work of conversion is understood to occur primarily in a communal rather than in an individual context. These three themes best characterize the Reformed theology of conversion.

CONVERSION IN THE
TWENTIETH-CENTURY CONTEXT

One of the most remarkable developments of the late twentieth century is telecommunication technology that has truly created a global village. Cultures and communities that were once remote and unknown are now only as far away as the television set, the telephone, or the computer. At the same time, modern transportation has promoted a degree of mobility in human society that could not have been imagined a century ago.

North America, in particular, is becoming increasingly a multicultural society—a mosaic of individuals and communities from a multitude of places on the globe. The encounter between different cultures, though by no means wholly new, is never easy or simple. History shows that such contacts often end in the suppression of one culture by another, either in outright war and genocide or in the domination of cultural symbols and memory. The unique situation of the late twentieth century is that the number of cross-cultural encounters has grown exponentially, and the old pattern of relating cultures (i.e., some dominant while others are submissive) is no longer deemed acceptable or even defensible to many Christians.

In theological studies these developments have resulted in an increasing focus on ecumenism, pluralism, and interfaith dialogue. Efforts around the turn of this century to create cooperative missionary outreach among the various Christian denominations eventually led to the formation of the World Council of Churches in 1948. Largely through its efforts, an ecumenical movement has emerged that has undercut confessional rivalry and mistrust among Christian churches. Proselytizing Christians from one denomination by another is now widely agreed to be inappropriate.[32] Although the goal of sharing full communion among Christian denominations still seems to be a remote outcome, today there is a degree of tolerance for the diversity of theological expressions of the one faith in Christ as God and Savior that is remarkable.

The meaning of pluralism for Christian theology extends beyond an acknowledgment of, and respect for, denominational diversity, however. The recognition that even within particular institutional or regional boundaries there is diversity of gender, ethnicity, culture, and race has led Christian theologians to recognize that culture informs the expression of Christian truth. Moreover, pluralism, if taken to mean competing truth claims, not varied expressions of a single truth, raises the question of the defensibility of Christianity's claims. Perhaps the most difficult agenda for Christian theology that emerges from its reflection on pluralism is the need to engage the truth claims made by other world religions in interfaith dialogue. This has been a major focus of recent writing by Christian theologians.[33]

But pluralism with all the challenges it presents to traditional Christian doctrine is not only a fact of modern existence, it is a reality with which theology must cope. Many would argue that pluralism is also an intellectual and ethical value that theology must promote.[34] It can hardly be overstated what a revolution this represents in the history of Christian thought and Western thought in general. The struggle to define orthodoxy, or "right belief," that so often dominated Christian theology, even in our own century, is grounded on a different premise: that truth, which is one, should have a single expression for all people.

These broad developments in recent theology raise difficult questions for the concept of conversion. Perhaps the most radical is the question whether attempts to convert others are in themselves acts of cultural violence.

There is certainly ample historical evidence that mass conversions, such as those of the barbarians in the late antique world and of the Indians of the Americas in the sixteenth and seventeenth centuries, were accompanied by the most appalling forms of literal physical violence. But even when Christians did not kill, enslave, or plunder the societies of their converts, we can discover more subtle forms of violence. The Puritans' attempt to bring Amerindians into their churches in colonial New England, for example, often led to a disturbing split consciousness in the minds of the converts. Because they were expected to recount their conversion in the same terms theologically and experientially as those of their European mentors, Amerindians were asked to deny the reality of their own experience of and language about the divine when it conflicted with standard Puritan theology.[35] Similarly, African-American slaves who received their induction into Christianity at the hands of their masters often suffered under an image of God that contributed further to their oppression.[36] Now it is certain that the Puritans and the slave masters believed they were simply disabusing their converts of false religion and providing them with the truth about God and salvation. But with the distance of historical observation, we can see how much cultural baggage was carried with these conversions. The very attempt to provide a group of people with a fully developed set of symbols for speaking about God and God's relation to the world—an attempt usually undertaken by those trying to convert others—betrays a kind of cultural arrogance that is a subtle form of violence.

The preceding discussion, of course, leads inevitably to the question of the absoluteness of Christianity. Do we have a truth that, in some form, is uniquely ours to share with others for their salvation? There is no way, within the limits of the present essay, that we can deal adequately with this difficult theological and philosophical question.[37] Nevertheless, it seems to me that the questions raised by pluralism ought at least to give us pause as we endeavor to understand conversion for our times.

What motives do we have as we seek to convert others? In what ways do we impose our own language, culture, and symbolism on others as we seek to convert them? And where should we look for prospective converts? These are difficult questions, to be sure, but ones that must be asked and answered as we attempt to rethink the church's mission in the modern world.

FIVE ELEMENTS OF A REFORMED THEOLOGY OF CONVERSION

What, then, can we as Presbyterian and Reformed Christians say about conversion as we look ahead to a new century? Does the doctrine of conversion have a place in our theology of grace and practice of evangelism? Certainly it does, but only as carefully defined both to honor our tradition's distinctive theology of grace and to address some of the problems presented by our contemporary pluralistic culture. Any contemporary Reformed theology that attempts to balance these concerns must include five elements.

1. Conversion is a divine gift.

Of course there is nothing particularly new about this thesis. It has been a common presupposition in all previous Reformed understandings of conversion.[38] First argued against the medieval notion of preparation for grace, the Reformed insistence on the prevenience of grace later played an equally important role in debates with the Arminians. But our insistence upon reasserting this thesis is not merely an act of historical preservation. As Friedrich Schleiermacher argued, Pelagianism, the belief that the will is not disabled by the taint of original sin, is one of the perennial heresies of Christianity, which reappears again and again in different guises.[39] The Reformed tradition makes its contribution in insisting (with Paul and Augustine) that the transformation of individuals and communities that is wrought by conversion is an act of God. Human beings cannot decide to convert but can only respond to God's work already begun in them.

2. Conversion is a continuing process.

The Reformed tradition has been uncomfortable both with the idea of decisive, once-and-for-all conversion and with the notion that humans are capable of perfection in this life.[40] The need for repentance, the call to return to God and to our covenantal responsibilities, is one repeated many times in the lives of individual Christians as well as in the life of the church as a whole. The altar call and the "decision for Christ" may have their place, but they by no means sum up the meaning of conversion in Reformed theology.

3. Conversion takes place within the church as a communal event.

This thesis is really a corollary of the two previous ones. If conversion is a divine gift, then it should be sought in the place where the body of Jesus Christ is present, that is, the church. Further, if conversion is a continuing process, structures must be in place to aid its development. Reformed theology maintains that the call to repent and return to God is sounded as often as the word is rightly preached and the sacraments are duly administered in the church. While *individuals* certainly hear God's call in this context, their conversions are not individual decisions or achievements, but are rather the process of their induction into, and their nurture and formation by, the community of faith.

4. Conversion is experienced and expressed in a variety of ways.

The process of conversion that takes place in the church is as variable as are the individuals who experience it. Personality types, family dynamics, education, culture, race, gender, and many other variables lead to a plurality both of experience and of expression of the gift of conversion. This variety, so far from being shunned, should be welcomed and celebrated in the church. Recognition of the variety of human testimony about conversion at least begins to address the context of pluralism in which contemporary Reformed theology finds itself.

5. Conversion is not the task but the "equipping" (cf. Eph. 4:12) of the church.

The work of conversion that is done by the Holy Spirit in the church is not an end in itself. Conversion nurtures individuals in the community of faith, reawakens them to the meaning of their life in that community, and calls them back when they stray, so that they can participate in the work of realizing God's purposes for the whole creation. A theology of conversion that focuses solely on the fate of individual souls or that seeks to fatten up the church's membership rolls to the end of institutional self-preservation is very misguided. Conversion is a call to mission: it is the means by which the church is made an effective ambassador of God's work of reconciliation in Christ (2 Cor. 5:20).[41]

CONCLUSION

What this initial outline means practically for the renewal of Reformed evangelism can only be sketched in brief within the limits of this essay. Nevertheless, it seems clear, first of all, that the role of the church in the process of conversion is to be faithful in its regular ministry. The word must be preached, the sacraments must be administered, people must be educated and nurtured in the life of faith, if conversion is ever to occur. It is through these ordinary means that the Holy Spirit brings conversion about.

Second, it would be misguided for the church to focus all its evangelistic efforts outside its own doors. If conversion is a process that occurs within the church, we ought to look for converts first within our own midst. Do *we* still hear the gospel in all its radical implications? Are *we* still faithful to God's call? It is the church itself that is in need of conversion—of returning to God and God's work. Finally, it is a great temptation to the church to get caught up in the business of conversion as an end in itself. Even the classical Reformed notion of conversion as repentance and faith does not sum up the church's mission. If the end sought is the salvation of individual souls, as in the tent meetings and missionary movements of the nineteenth century, or the preservation of the institutional church in the face of declining membership, as in the church growth movement of our own day, the hard fact is that, even more, conversion must not become the ultimate goal.

The Reformed tradition has always insisted that the chief and highest end of human existence is not personal or institutional survival, but the glory of God. As Calvin wrote in his response to Cardinal Sadoleto:

> It is not very sound theology to confine a man's thoughts so much to himself, and not to set before him, as the prime motive of his existence, zeal to illustrate the glory of God. For we are born first of all for God, and not for ourselves. . . . This zeal ought to exceed all thought and care for our own good and advantage, and since natural equity also teaches that God does not receive what is his own, unless he is preferred to all things, it certainly is the part of a Christian man to ascend higher than merely to seek and secure the salvation of his own soul. I am persuaded, therefore, that there is no man imbued with true piety, who will not consider as insipid that long and laboured exhortation to zeal for heavenly life, a zeal which keeps a man entirely devoted to himself, and does not, even by one expression, arouse him to sanctify the name of God.[42]

NOTES

The author gratefully acknowledges the helpful suggestions and criticisms given to earlier drafts of this essay by Milton J Coalter, John Burkhart, and Brian Gerrish.

1. In the *Book of Confessions,* only the Second Helvetic Confession and the Westminster Confession of Faith and catechisms use the actual word "conversion," but they do not specify its precise meaning. *The Constitution*

of the Presbyterian Church (U.S.A.), Part I: *Book of Confessions* (Louisville, Ky.: Office of the General Assembly, 1991), 5.093–.094, 6.062, 7.089, 7.269.

2. There is a massive literature on the concept of religious conversion, and I cannot hope to engage even a fraction of it within the limits of this essay. For an excellent overview of the literature, see Lewis R. Rambo, "Current Research on Religious Conversion," *Religious Studies Review* 8 (1982): 146–59. For a good discussion of the issues of definition, see Lewis R. Rambo, "Conversion," in *The Encyclopedia of Religion,* ed. Mircea Eliade (New York and London: Macmillan Publishing Co., 1987), 4:73–79.

3. This, I take it, is what Rambo tries to do in defining conversion as "a dynamic, multifaceted process of change." "Conversion," 73.

4. Much has been written about the meaning and use of these terms that cannot be discussed within the limits of the present essay. For more extensive discussions, see Gerhard Kittel and Gerhard Friedrich, eds., *Theological Dictionary of the New Testament,* trans. Geoffrey W. Bromiley (Grand Rapids: Wm. B. Eerdmans Publishing Co., 1964–1976), 7:722–29, 4:975–1008. For more on the biblical concept of conversion, see Michael H. Crosby, "The Biblical Vision of Conversion," in *The Human Experience of Conversion: Persons and Structures in Transformation,* ed. Francis A. Eigo (Villanova, Pa.: Villanova University Press, 1987), 31–74. See also Dom Marc-François Lacan, "Conversion and Grace in the Old Testament," and "Conversion and Kingdom in the Synoptic Gospels," in *Conversion: Perspectives on Personal and Social Transformation,* ed. Walter E. Conn (New York: Alba House, 1978), 75–118; Hugh T. Kerr and John M. Mulder, eds., *Conversions: The Christian Experience* (Grand Rapids: Wm. B. Eerdmans Publishing Co., 1983), ix–xi.

5. Some recent biblical scholarship argues that Israel's origin was the result of a conversion. See Norman Gottwald, *The Tribes of Yahweh: A Sociology of the Religion of Liberated Israel, 1250–1050 B.C.E.* (Maryknoll, N.Y.: Orbis Books, 1981).

6. The examples of David's conviction of sin as presented in 2 Samuel 12 or the prophet's vision of the Lord in Isaiah 6 suggest a more decisive moment of conversion.

7. Despite the example of Paul's conversion as told by Luke, Paul's own discussion of transformation emphasizes gradual growth and is suspicious of excessive emotionalism. See Alan F. Segal, *Paul the Convert: The Apostolate and Apostasy of Saul the Pharisee* (New Haven, Conn.: Yale University Press, 1990), 106–14. The question whether Paul even experienced a conversion has been debated. See Krister Stendahl, *Paul among the Jews and Gentiles* (Philadelphia: Fortress Press, 1976), 7–23.

8. Crosby, "Biblical Vision," 56–60.

9. Segal, *Paul,* 67–68. Paul's vision of cosmic redemption is perhaps more clearly expressed in Romans 8.19–23.

10. An excellent collection of conversion stories may be found in *Conversions,* edited by Kerr and Mulder. See also James Craig Holte, ed., *The*

Conversion Experience in America: A Sourcebook on Religious Conversion Autobiography (New York: Greenwood Press, 1992).

11. In *Conversions,* xii, Kerr and Mulder note that conversion stories are virtually absent during the whole of the Middle Ages. They suggest that of the mass conversions after the time of Constantine many would have been inauthentic. They also suggest that conversion stories used for the purpose of persuading others would have been part of an oral rather than a written culture. But there is a further *theological* reason for the lack of conversion stories and theologies in the medieval period. The Roman Church's penitential system largely defined the theology of grace in the Middle Ages, and it was concerned not with a decisive moment of transformation but with an ever-repeating cycle of sin-confession-satisfaction.

12. See, for example, John Bunyan, *Grace Abounding to the Chief of Sinners* (1666).

13. Jerald C. Brauer, "Conversion: From Puritanism to Revivalism," *Journal of Religion* 58 (1978): 234.

14. Ibid., 241–43.

15. For an example of this, see Charles Grandison Finney, *True and False Repentance: Evangelistic Messages* (Grand Rapids: Kregel Publications, 1966), 11–51.

16. Bernard Lonergan, *Insight: A Study of Human Understanding* (London: Longmans, Green & Co.; New York: Philosophical Library, 1957); Francis A. Eigo, ed., *Human Experience;* Donald L. Gelpi, *Charism and Sacrament: A Theology of Christian Conversion* (New York: Paulist Press, 1976), and *Experiencing God: A Theology of Human Emergence* (New York: Paulist Press, 1978); see also Walter Conn, *Christian Conversion: A Developmental Interpretation of Autonomy and Surrender* (Mahwah, N.J.: Paulist Press, 1986).

17. For a discussion of the few instances in which Calvin uses the word "conversion," see T.H.L. Parker's article on conversion in Alan Richardson, ed., *A Dictionary of Christian Theology* (London: SCM Press, 1969), 73–75.

18. *Calvin: Institutes of the Christian Religion,* ed. John T. McNeill, trans. Ford Lewis Battles, The Library of Christian Classsics, Vols. 20 and 21 (Philadelphia: Westminster Press, 1960), 3.3.1.

19. *Institutes,* 3.3.5; see also John Calvin, *Commentary on Acts* 26.19, *Ioannis Calvini opera quae supersunt omnia,* ed. W. Baum, E. Cunitz, E. Reuss (Braunschweig and Berlin: C. A. Schwetschke & Son, 1865–1900), vol. 48, col. 544.

20. *Institutes,* 3.10–15.

21. *ᵣ· ᵤitutes,* 3.4.1.

22. *Institutes,* 3.3.9.

23. *Institutes,* 3.3.21.

24. See Brian A. Gerrish, *Grace and Gratitude: The Eucharistic Theology of John Calvin* (Minneapolis: Fortress Press, 1992), 94–95.

25. It was Calvin's reference to Ephesians 2:10 in his discussion in *Institutes*, 3.3.21, that led me to use this text as one of my epigraphs.

26. *Book of Confessions*, 5.093–.105.

27. Ibid.

28. *Book of Confessions*, 6.064. For Calvin on calling, see *Institutes*, 3.24.

29. *Book of Confessions*, 6.083.

30. Friedrich Schleiermacher (1768–1834), for example, takes regeneration to be the encompassing term of which conversion and justification are constituent parts. Conversion, he argues, consists of repentance and faith. See *Der christliche Glaube nach den Grundsätzen der evangelischen Kirche im Zusammenhange dargestellt* (1821–22; 2d ed., 1830–31); Eng. trans. *The Christian Faith*, trans. from the 2d German ed. by H. R. Mackintosh and J. S. Stewart [Philadelphia: Fortress Press, 1976], §§107–109. Heinrich Heppe (1820–1879) speaks of faith as the effect of regeneration and conversion, both of which are subsumed under effectual calling, while the doctrines of justification and sanctification are treated separately. See *Die Dogmatik der evangelische reformierten Kirche, dargestellt und aus den Quellen belegt* (Elberfeld: Friderichs, 1861), Loc. XX, pp. 367–92; Eng. trans. *Reformed Dogmatics*, trans. G. T. Thomson, ed. Ernst Bizer [London: George Allen & Unwin, 1950]. Charles Hodge (1797–1878) treats regeneration, faith, and justification as discrete doctrines. He speaks of conversion under the rubric of regeneration but identifies it as the human response to God's act in regeneration. *Systematic Theology* (New York: Scribner, Armstrong, 1874), vol. 3, chap. 15. Even these few examples demonstrate, I think, how complicated it is to sort out the language of soteriology even in one confessional tradition. But the broad agreement in substance among these three theologians is in insisting on the prevenience of grace and the need to see faith as the effect of grace rather than its cause.

31. Schleiermacher states it succinctly: "No example can be given of conversion apart from the mediation of the word: and we need cherish no misgiving that to assert this strenuously is to limit the divine omnipotence." *Christian Faith*, §108.5.

32. See the document prepared by the Joint Working Group between the Roman Catholic Church and the World Council of Churches, *Common Witness and Proselytism* (Geneva: World Council of Churches, 1970).

33. The literature one could cite here is also enormous. For a discussion of Christology by a theologian engaged in Christian/Buddhist dialogue, see John B. Cobb, Jr., *Christ in a Pluralistic Age* (Philadelphia: Westminster Press, 1975). See also John B. Cobb, *Beyond Dialogue: Toward a Mutual Transformation of Christianity and Buddhism* (Philadelphia: Fortress Press, 1982); Langdon Brown Gilkey, *Through the Tempest: Theological Voyages in a Pluralistic Culture*, sel. and ed. Jeff B. Pool (Minneapolis: Fortress Press, 1991); David Tracy, *Plurality and Ambiguity: Hermeneutics, Religion, Hope* (New York: Harper & Row, 1987).

34. Schubert M. Ogden makes this point in his entry on "Pluralism" in *The Westminster Dictionary of Christian Theology,* ed. Alan Richardson and John Bowden (Philadelphia: Westminster Press, 1983), 449–51. One could argue that the current explosion of theologies from many perspectives—feminist, womanist, Korean, Hispanic, African, etc.—confirms Ogden's observation that pluralism is taken as a value. Many contemporary theologians maintain that diversity not only in denominational affiliation but also in race, gender, culture, nationality, education, etc., ought to be represented in systematic construction. See, for example, Susan Brooks Thistlethwaite and Mary Potter Engel, eds., *Lift Every Voice: Constructing Christian Theologies from the Underside* (San Francisco: Harper, 1990).

35. I was instructed on this point by an unpublished paper presented at a University of Chicago history seminar by Charles L. Cohen, "Conversion among the Puritans and Amerindians: A Theological and Cultural Perspective." See also Charles L. Cohen, *God's Caress: The Psychology of Puritan Religious Experience* (New York: Oxford University Press, 1986).

36. See the fascinating discussion of this point in Alice Walker's novel *The Color Purple* (New York: Washington Square Press, 1982), 176–77.

37. The classic discussion of this problem remains Ernst Troeltsch, *The Absoluteness of Christianity and the History of Religions,* trans. David Reid (Richmond: John Knox Press, 1971). However, contemporary theologians continue to wrestle with this difficult issue. See, for example, Schubert M. Ogden, *Is There Only One True Religion or Are There Many?* (Dallas: Southern Methodist University Press, 1992).

38. This, I take it, is the point being made in the passage from Karl Barth's *Church Dogmatics* that I used as an epigraph to this chapter. Karl Barth, *Church Dogmatics,* ed. G. W. Bromiley and T. F. Torrance, trans. G. W. Bromiley (Edinburgh: T. & T. Clark, 1958), IV/2, 579.

39. Schleiermacher, *Christian Faith,* §22.

40. Interestingly, there seems to be a convergence in the conclusions of studies of conversion in several disciplines that suggests that the moment of conversion is only one dramatic part of a long-term process. See Holte, *Conversion Experience,* x.

41. Karl Barth states this point powerfully: "The biblical individual is not selfishly wrapped up in his own concerns. . . . His conversion and renewal is not, therefore, an end in itself, as it has often been interpreted and represented in a far too egocentric Christianity. The man who wants to be converted only for his own sake and for himself rather than to God the Lord and to entry into the service of His cause on earth and as His witness in the cosmos is not the whole man. When we convert and are renewed in the totality of our being, we cross the threshold of our private existence and move out into the open. The inner problems may be most urgent and burning and exciting, but we are not engaged in conversion if we confine ourselves to them. We simply run (in a rather more subtle way) on our own path

headlong to destruction. When we convert and are renewed in the totality of our being, in and with our private responsibility we also accept a public responsibility. For it is the great God of heaven and earth who is for us, and we are for this God" (*Church Dognatics,* IV/2, 565).

42. *Calvin's Tracts and Treatises,* trans. Henry Beveridge, 7 vols. (reprint ed., Grand Rapids: Baker Book House, 1983), 1:33–34. Here, as elsewhere, Calvin does of course say that God commends the highest end to us by making our salvation depend on it. But the priority is clear.

3. Evangelism and Education: Making Disciples Reformed

DAVID C. HESTER

In the Great Commission at the end of Matthew's Gospel, evangelism and education are inextricably linked as complementary movements in the rhythm of disciple making. The risen Christ, in Matthew's text, commands his disciples, "Go . . . and make disciples . . . , baptizing them . . . , teaching them to obey everything that I have commanded you. And remember, I am with you always" (Matt. 28:19–20). Those who encounter Christ in his disciples' proclamation of the gospel are invited to confess Christ as Lord and Savior, to be joined to Christ's body through baptism, to learn to live as Christ's disciples in the world, and to continue the rhythm of love and disciple making. In this process, evangelism, worship, education, and mission are experienced as an ecological whole—the rich soil in which discipleship grows and bears its fruit.

The relationship between evangelism and education in Reformed traditions has echoed faithfully this ancient ecology. Even a quick scan of denominational documents over the years reveals the intimate connection between calling persons to Christ, inviting them to membership, and teaching one another to walk in the Spirit of Christ amid constantly changing life circumstances.

Education, in Reformed tradition, is believed to be directed by the Spirit in service to discipleship. Thus, learning is *learning how to live as disciples,* evidencing in our lives the confession we have made in response to the word we received. Education is learning how to proclaim the gospel in word and deed, while living in the gospel's grace in the company of others bound to follow Christ. Or, to put it differently, in Reformed practice, education is the nurture and direction necessary for conversion, to centering life in Christ.

47

Education participates in our reorientation to the One in whose image we are made and in the transformation of our values and patterns of daily life that is necessary to "walk in the Spirit" as people of "new creation" in Christ. This conversion experience is ongoing: it is the changing of our mind into the mind of Christ that begins with a claim to follow Christ and continues against the constant temptation to think otherwise and to follow other "principalities and powers" that dwell within us and around us.

Evangelism, in Reformed tradition, is the church's work of proclaiming the gospel in word and deed, inviting persons to participate in the grace of God and to join in the mutual care and public ministry of the community of God's covenant people. It is therefore a work intended both for those outside the community, the unbaptized, and for those within the community, since disobedience puts us regularly "outside" the community metaphorically by reason of our failure to live into our baptism in the Spirit.

Evangelism, too, is ongoing activity; it happens whenever and wherever the gospel is proclaimed and heard and Christ is perceived in the world. It happens in worship; it goes on when the hungry are fed, the lonely visited, the mournful comforted, and justice done for the poor in Christ's name. Evangelism is the gospel present when forgiveness restores relationships in Christ's name, when children are loved and protected, and when work becomes a means for participating in God's redemptive activity in the world, rather than a way to earn a living.

This does not mean that evangelism is everything we do in Christ's name. The point, rather, is that we proclaim the gospel in a variety of ways. Where we do so consciously and intentionally, with the purpose of witnessing to Christ and inviting the children of God to share in Christ's body, we are engaged in evangelism.

The connective tissue between evangelism and education is clear: if evangelism invites persons into the community of Christ, church education equips us to live together faithfully in Christ, as Christ's disciples. We learn how to love one another as Christ has loved us and how to love our neighbors as ourselves publicly. Education is the intentional activity of the community of faith that enables persons to walk in the Spirit after Christ and "so fulfill the law of God" that redemptive love and divine justice may be experienced in all quarters of our life in anticipation of the consummation of the reign of God. It assumes that participants wish to pursue a lifestyle in conformity with the desire of God, empowered by the Spirit of God. It assumes that the practice of such a lifestyle is learned behavior and that life together as a community of faith is the primary means and locus for the education of Christians.

In this essay, we will look at three evangelical roles of educational ministry: education for belonging (initiation), education for critical reflection (life in the Spirit), and education for public transformation (the life of public witness). The goal in the first role is identity formation; the aim of the second role is identity re-formation; and the purpose in the third role is public persuasion or identity sharing (testimony).

Education for belonging recognizes that the gospel calls us into a community of faith. This community has a distinctive and identity-giving history, particular ways of being and doing, special symbols and rituals, and a variety of related but not necessarily identical beliefs. We learn how we belong in such a community; we learn *to belong* by learning the community's shared history, its sacred texts with their vision of the future, the significance and power of its sacred symbols, and how to participate in its rituals of worship, celebration, and restoration. If education for belonging is effective, those initiated by baptism will *know themselves* as disciples of Christ who belong to both the communion of saints spanning the ages and a local congregation of brothers and sisters in Christ.

The evangelical role of *education for critical reflection* recognizes that the Spirit pushes us to interpret the contemporary world and our personal situations in the light of the gospel of Christ. As the Reformation motto puts it, we are "always being reformed" by the Spirit. Education for critical reflection teaches us to look for Christ "with us," present in the world to redeem it. It teaches us to look for the "new thing" God is doing in our day. It teaches us to recognize sin in our personal and communal life and our culpability for it. It teaches us to examine what we believe, to ask ourselves about the ways we articulate our relationship to God in Christ. It teaches us how we can best express the meaning and truth we see in the gospel in language that is continuous with our traditions yet communicates with people who are largely secular in their language and outlook.

Finally, *education for public transformation* recognizes that the gospel is world changing as well as person changing. It teaches us that the gospel proclaims a way of justice and love that is intended to bless all creation and not the disciples of Christ alone. The way of Christ is the way of fully human life. Therefore, it is our responsibility to place the gospel's vision for the good life in public forums as realistic alternatives for shaping social life. In this context, the Christian community learns to be exemplary of the love and justice we believe appropriate to the happiness and welfare of every community, regardless of whether others are motivated to join the Christian community as disciples themselves. This evangelical role of education looks carefully within our traditions for the universal grounds for human hope and meaning in Christ's story. These offer a re-creation of human life in community in the image of God.

EDUCATION FOR BELONGING
(INITIATION AND FORMATION)

Early in the church's history of disciple making, the formative concerns of education were addressed to adults who already belonged to social groups that gave them their identity. Then as now, the sources on which persons drew for their identity—their values, worldview, and personal history—were complex. They included family ties, citizenship or social/cultural ties, and religious community affiliations. Initiation into the Christian community involved not only conversion from sin—a lifestyle of obedience to what Paul called "principalities and powers of this present evil age"—but also a turning away from family members and community groups that had once been home or at least the source of social identity—the place of belonging.[1]

The rites and symbols associated with adult baptism were intended to symbolize a turning away from an old lifestyle and a turning to (the rest of the meaning of conversion) a new community of identity and belonging. Renunciation of old ways, stripping away of old clothes, affirmation of new loyalty and understanding shared with the new community, together with participation in the transforming experience of dying and rising with Christ in the baptismal water were all intended to carry the baptized from one way of living to another, from one communal orientation to another. Family ties remained but were now qualified by belonging to the family of all whose brother is Christ and whose true parent is the delivering God who sent Christ into the world. Social and cultural marks, such as one's origin, social experiences, and benefits of education, class, or citizenship, inevitably remained. But these too were now qualified by both a oneness in service to Christ and the ironic equality of becoming subject to public persecution.

Baptismal creeds, such as that preserved in Philippians 2 and the later Apostles' Creed, indicate basic acknowledgments that were required in order to belong to the baptized community. These statements of faith indicate more than required doctrine; they convey the fundamental outlines of the community's shared story. These the initiated must learn, literally, by heart. From this community of memory the initiate would draw her or his identity, proclaiming the story of the community as "our story" and confessing essential beliefs as "my" beliefs. Preparation for baptism focused on helping converts reinterpret their life experiences in the light of the new Christian story. It involved teaching them to see a familiar world in an unfamiliar, radically different way, while providing them a community of support and nurture to aid their successful conversion into a new community.

Things have changed considerably in our world of the American church. We live in a society that, though now thoroughly transformed by the rationalistic and scientific emphases of the modern age, was founded on principles rooted in the biblical traditions of Judaism and Christianity and particularly Christianity as expressed through the churches of the Reformation.

Christianity is a part of the American cultural experience. This does not mean that the United States is or ever has been a Christian nation. It does mean, however, that the Christian tradition has made important contributions to the principles undergirding our national documents of independence and constitution. It has also shaped the perspective of generations of Americans whose loyalty to country was affirmed within the larger context of loyalty to the Creator and Sustainer of all nations and peoples.

In this context, becoming Christian has happened within a society that welcomed and even expected such conversion to take place. By contrast with the early church, being non-Christian in our culture has been exceptional and being Christian—even if only vaguely so—has been the rule.

The Reformed experience has been very much like that of other mainline denominations. We have tended to grow from the inside out, so to speak, with membership increases coming largely from children of members, baptized as infants and confirmed as full members sometime in adolescence. Or new members joined, having belonged first to another Christian communion but now becoming Reformed or Presbyterian because of a marriage, a change in neighborhood, or a change in religious beliefs.[2] Thus, declining birthrates and delayed marriages have contributed to mainstream membership decline.

This pattern has not been the wrenching experience of conversion so typical of the first Christian communities, which literally made new Christians outcasts from their former communities of identity. Rather, conversion in the Reformed experience has involved personal transformation that offered a distinctive perspective on life in which to see one's past, present, and future—an important, significant, orienting time in one's life but not one that marginalized the believer from the mainstream of society.[3]

This is not to say that dramatic conversion experiences are at all foreign to the Reformed experience. Conversion, however experienced, is always life changing and soul shaping. But, typically, the conversion experience for American Reformed Christians has been an extended, growing experience of coming to see clearly and explicitly what one has formerly known vaguely and implicitly.

Our practice of infant baptism, indeed, has affirmed that our children are initiated into the body of Christ at birth, as children of adult believers themselves living into their baptism as disciples of Christ and members of a church community. The model implicit in this practice affirms that the evangelization of children begins within the Christian family, which is in turn supported and nurtured within a community of faith. The education question focuses first on the educational needs of children in their families and of families in the church. To put it more directly, in this model the education question is How do we intentionally initiate children who are baptized into the community of faith so that they know themselves to belong to Christ and Christ's community, identifying themselves with the shared memory of the Christian community and practicing a lifestyle that indicates and reinforces their belonging in Christ? How do we teach baptized children to see reality from the perspective of living in the body of Christ, so that their mind is not conformed to "this world" but rather "transformed" in order to "discern what is the will of God—what is good and acceptable and perfect" (Rom. 12:2)?

But things have changed. The truth is that any model of evangelism that assumes today that parenting adults will bring their children for baptism and are prepared to nurture them "in the Lord" is misreading the signs of the times. Mainline church studies confirm what we know anecdotally: American young adults are not in church on Sunday morning, and many of them did not grow up in homes where belonging to church meant active participation in congregational life. In the past, young adults have typically dropped out for a time and returned to congregations when children are born. But there is little reason to conclude that the so-called baby boomers' children will return as adults or that their homes offer a self-consciously Christian nurture.

We have a new set of conditions for initiation: we are concerned not only with an evangelism that initiates baptized children into full community participation and a lifestyle of discipleship but with a generation of adults, some baptized as infants, who must be taught to belong too. Our discussion, then, must attend to evangelism for initiation appropriate for children, in harmony with our historical practice of infant baptism, and evangelism for initiation appropriate for adults, whose heritage may be Christian but whose commitments and sense of identity are practically secular.

We may focus on the children, some of whom come to church these days with their parents, some with grandparents, some with neighborhood friends, and some simply come alone. How shall we teach them that God welcomes them to the covenant people of God? The essentials we discover here would be appropriate for initiating adults, too, though necessarily adjusted to reflect adult thinking abilities, feelings, and behavior. "Children of God," after all, is a favorite metaphor for all of us who belong in Christ, whether we are chronologically young or older. Children, as Jesus suggested, can be effective teachers for all of us.

The history of the nineteenth-century Sunday school movement exemplifies the close connection between evangelism and education for children throughout the church's history.[4] The mission of American Sunday schools, particularly on the frontier, was twofold. It sought to provide moral education and catechetical instruction in preparation for an anticipated experience of spiritual awakening, and it tried to offer education necessary for reading the Bible and other documents of faith essential to a Christian life "worthy of repentance." That same spirit of interdependency is reflected in the encouragement found in a Christian Education Committee Report to the General Assembly of 1947 that ascribes to each teacher the role of "an evangelist."[5] If children were to live a good, Christian life, it was up to the Sunday school to instill the knowledge necessary. Furthermore, it was expected that this work would be reinforced by family and a culture dominated by a Protestant ethos.

The evangelical focus of Protestant Sunday school education was modified by two simultaneous developments: a commitment on the part of Reformed communions and others to a historical-critical approach to biblical interpretation, and the "takeover" of the Sunday school movement by a theologically liberal and educationally progressive approach to "religious education." The latter focused on the learning needs of children and assumed a natural progression of spiritual development.[6]

Both of these factors complicated Bible teaching enormously. As the common or public school took over the goal of teaching reading and writing, the Sunday school shifted more and more attention to the broad themes of Christian living and learning about the Bible—its history, the history of its ancient people, and its content helpful to developing a good Christian life. The development of more complex goals and sensitivity to age-related needs and appropriate developmental skills brought with it more highly developed and sophisticated church school curricula. Evangelical commitments became more subtle and the background to specific and apparent objectives associated with learning to live as a Christian. In the process, the Sunday school lost its sharp evangelical focus.

The evangelical emphasis of Christian education can be faithfully reformed by recognizing the full range of ways in which children encounter the gospel of Jesus Christ and are invited to participate in God's grace. The revivalist tactics of earlier efforts may no longer be appropriate for our children, but that does not mean the surrender of the conscientious evangelization of children by and in the community of faith. Indeed, the pledge we make at their baptism—to raise them to know Christ as Lord and Savior—is a commitment to evangelize them, and it is expected that the gospel will be proclaimed to them in the words and deeds of their families and their congregation. These are the significant places where they may come to know Christ and know themselves as persons called to be Christ's disciples.

Children come to know Christ first through the witness to Christ's love and care for them demonstrated and interpreted by loving parents and caring adult friends. We have long recognized the significance for children of their early experiences in the home and the congregation. This is the context wherein they learn trust, hope, self-discipline, and love for themselves and for others. But we sometimes talk and act as if these were simply human virtues to be nurtured experientially with children too young to go to school and really learn. By this we mean apparently cognitive achievement primarily; learning to think and learning information. The fact is that if children encounter Christ, they do so, like the rest of us, primarily in the lives of people witnessing to Christ by loving like Christ, by healing like Christ, by offering hope and help like Christ, by forgiving one another like Christ, and by remaining trustworthy like Christ. The school for this encounter with Christ is only incidentally a classroom. The primary setting is family and congregational life with their myriad opportunities for witnessing the way of Christ and the grace of God. If immediate family is not available for children to experience the witness of Christ's love, as seems to be the case frequently these days, then congregational witness becomes all the more critical and essential.

The biblical texts and doctrinal texts children "read" and "interpret" most formatively are the storied lives of parents, adults, and other children. Their interaction with others provides the context for meaningful questions and responses—implicit and explicit—through which Christ is made known.[7] Christ and the gospel of Christ is encountered first as the witness of others to Christ, and what is true for children, in fact, is true for all of us at any age. But children, most of all, are dependent on others to interpret the meaning of the way things are and why we live the way we do. Children learn first as precritical thinkers, trusting the reality they experience and the truthfulness of their intimate teachers. Our witness to Christ and the Christian life, therefore, is especially critical and powerful with young children; we are the gospel they hear and see preeminently.

Initiating children into a life of Christian faith, then, requires the conscious witnessing of parents and other adults to the gospel of Christ in the context of everyday living patterns, where lives touch and are formed and reformed as children grow toward maturity. *Conscious witnessing* means anticipating opportunities for interpreting children's experience in the light of God's grace and Christ's redemptive love. Children naturally and enthusiastically ask questions about meaning, about how and why things happen as they experience them. These questions, for Christian witnesses, find their deepest and best answers in the character of God, the gift of love in Christ, and the hope we have in Christ for God's future new creation.

But these responses do not come naturally for Christian parents and adults. They must be learned and constructed circumstantially if they are to interpret children's experiences persuasively, honestly, and without dogmatic oversimplification. To talk of what we see and do with the mind of Christ: that is our teaching requirement here. But we must do so in ways that honor the cognitive and affective capabilities of children, while conveying the truth of the gospel's understanding of reality, perceived through the witness of biblical texts.

Adults working together to learn how to interpret children's experiences and questions in the light of the life and purpose of Christ, while providing mutual support for their witnessing, is an essential educational task and opportunity for which congregations need to provide space and resources.

Specific possibilities come to mind. One example is the Louisville Presbyterian congregation that gathered parents to participate in case study discussions around typical family events involving their children. Participants asked in each case how their Christian faith might inform what they do and say in that context so that their children may see that Christian faith makes a difference in how we behave and the choices we make.

Whatever the format, the focus is helping parents and adults become interpreters to children of their life experiences, so that they may encounter Christ through the witness of Christian parents and friends in the midst of their everyday life. Christ becomes visible and vital to our children through the living witnesses we are as parenting adults. We are the body of Christ into which they have been received. Our life together, interpreted by our ongoing witness to the gospel story, must build upon their natural sense of belonging with us, inviting them to *choose* to belong, to acknowledge for themselves that with Christ in the community of Christ's disciples they are "at home."

This conscious community witness is critical, as well, for adult initiates. Congregations need to plan ways to intentionally teach seekers and newcomers ways of being Christian in a particular community, that is, the ways of community care for one another, the ways of worship together, and the ways of joining in the congregation's mission of loving service. A new-members class is not enough. The educational effort to initiate must be more involving in the life of the congregation than that. A mentoring or apprentice model is a more appropriate approach for adults learning to belong to the body of Christ.

If we want children to come to belong in the body of Christ, at least two other evangelical concerns deserve our attention. The gospel is not only the lens through which we see our experiences in full dimension; it is also the sacred repository of our Christian and Reformed community's founding story and guide for practices that distinguish our belonging to this particular community of faith. Evangelical education means teaching our children the gospel story as our faith community's essential identity story and teaching them the practices drawn from that story that are essential for Christian life. I have in mind here the kind of nonnegotiable matters of our faith that serve as Christian instruction or, as in Judaism, our Torah.[8] In Reformed theology, Christ is our Torah, our Law and the Prophets. Nevertheless, the scriptures—Old and New Testaments— bear witness in essential ways to Christ and thereby have become for us the means of God's self-revelation—"Word of God written," in the language of the Confession of 1967. Therefore, to belong to the body of Christ requires appropriating the community's founding gospel story, so that the "they" of the story's witnesses becomes "we" in its subsequent retelling.[9]

Educationally, then, a congregation must answer the question, What in our traditions and practices is essential for our children and for initiates of any age to know so that they belong, authentically and responsibly, to this community of faith? Most would agree that knowing the Bible is fundamental to our identity as Christian disciples. But interpreting the Bible is a lifelong process, and we are concerned here with essential knowledge for belonging and beginning discipleship. Where should we start?

Our answer will depend on how we see our identity revealed to us through the Bible texts. The child's first question is not Who is God? or What must I believe? or even How did the church come into being? The child's first question is our own first question, Who am I? and the related question, How can I understand everything that I am experiencing? This first question is one of meaning and, specifically, meaning posed as a question arising from an awareness of a self experiencing an environment of feelings, needs, and others.[10] The answer we want to offer children in Christ is this: you are a child of God, created in God's love, living in relationship with God so gracefully that "nothing can separate us from the love of God in Christ." You are "one of us," belonging to the family of God, brothers and sisters of one another and of Christ. Christ has entrusted us all in this community of faith with your care, your nurture, and with loving you with God's love. You are called by God in Christ to live with us as people of God showing in all you do the love of God in Christ for the whole world.

The Bible tells us and our children that we are like this and that we belong to God always by telling us about a child born to parents seeking to live as people of God long ago. This child is both like us and different. He is like us because he knows our fears, needs, and deepest questions; he is different because God chose him to live as the full and undistorted image of God—the way God intends for all of us—and because through him and the experiences of his life, God revealed the depth of God's love and the height of God's hope for full and joyful life for each and all of us and for the whole creation. This is Jesus the Christ's story; this is the place we begin. It is not, to be sure, where the "good news of God's grace" begins, since God's evangel is hovering over the opening words of creation in Genesis. But the story of Jesus the Christ is the identity-forming story of the Christian community. It is the light in which we reread and reappropriate the gospel encountered first by Israel, which has become our Hebrew Scriptures tradition. For us, for our community of faith, we know what it means to belong to God because we know that we have been claimed by God in Christ and called through Christ into the community of God's people, the family of God's beloved children.

It is essential, then, that we know and teach the story of Jesus the Christ to those who would belong with us. I want to emphasize the narrative character of what we need to teach here: it is Jesus' life story, together with his teaching, that constitutes our community's foundation. But it is life story, not biography, I have in mind. Modern thought conceives of biography as a historical, descriptive process, guided by primary historical documents, methods of research verification, and critical and analytical reporting by the biographer. The sources we have for Jesus' life story—the New Testament Gospels, primarily—do not fit this modern genre. In the context of the written Gospels, Jesus' life story and teachings constitute what Jesus is said to have said by the community's witnesses. We tell this story always mindful of the historical problems and questions that attend it. But our identity as Christians is not dependent on historical validation of Jesus' biography or Jesus' words. It is dependent on first receiving and knowing the story as the handed-on witness of Christian disciples. This witness has served to reform the community of faith as witnesses in each generation. This retelling and reforming the story goes on among new people encountering familiar questions of meaning in constantly changing circumstances. It becomes "gospel" for a new generation as modern people encounter the truth of Christ through the power of the Holy Spirit interpreting their present situations.

The most fundamental way to frame this gospel story, so that it may be learned by heart, is by liturgical practice, rather than as classroom curricula. The implication is that if we want to do evangelical education for children, they need to be an active part of community worship and liturgy. Moreover, we need to create additional liturgical moments at home. This would include opportunities to recite the gospel story around dinner tables, on occasions of holiday gathering, and at poignant times of change and transition in the life of the family. Such occasions occur, for example, when children leave for summer visits, end the school year or begin another, lose or gain a pet, greet a new sibling, celebrate a birthday or the anniversary of their baptism. If it is desirable for Christian families to pay attention to the seasons of the Christian year, surely it could be helpful to create a ritual or liturgical cycle such as this for the seasons of family and individual life.

When the community gathers for worship, more time needs to be provided for recounting the full story of Christ on occasion, rather than hearing the story piecemeal through the lectionary selections only. For example, the First Sunday of Advent could be an occasion for recalling the full gospel story, compressed as it might be in time allowed. There are examples at hand in the New Testament itself of earlier efforts to encapsule the story for specific occasions of telling (e.g., the sermons in Acts). Indeed, the framework of the Synoptic Gospels would seem to provide guidance, since they include Jesus' hoped-for birth in the context of a suffering world, his call to ministry, words and deeds of the gospel he preached and became, and his passion, death, and resurrection. Once this framework is formed in memory, then the educational task can be extended to fill it out, both with detail and, eventually, with critical reflection mindful of historical-critical insights about the development of the tradition over the life of the church. The story of Israel as well as the content and insight of the Hebrew Scriptures are thus joined to the Christ story as testimony to the steadfast love of God from "the beginning," the context for understanding the "new" in Christ. Attention to teaching the gospel of the Bible in liturgical contexts will require particular concern for these opportunities for inclusion of God's good news from the Hebrew Scriptures, as testimony to the love of God and the desire of God for the healing and wholeness of all creation and not simply as texts anticipating the events of Christ's life.

Those who belong to Christ must also learn to live in Christ, that is, to live within the story they have learned to tell. The Bible calls this life of discipleship "life in the Spirit." This designation recognizes that belonging to Christ changes the whole environment in which we live. We see things differently because they really have changed in Christ, and the Spirit of God is present with us to empower us to live alternatively, too.[11]

The signs of our "new age" lifestyle in Christ are named in such places as the Ordinances of the church of the Presbyterian Church (U.S.A.)'s *Book of Order.*[12] Through these activities the grace of God may be experienced and followers of Christ may participate in the ministry of Christ in the world. These activities include worshiping together, telling the Christian story to one another, interpreting scriptures together, praying, confessing to and forgiving one another, encouraging one another in work and vocation, doing specific acts of faithful service and witness together, suffering with and for each other, and providing hospitality and care for one another and particularly for strangers. This is a partial list, of course. But all these activities must be learned and may be learned if the community consciously provides opportunities for learning an evangelical lifestyle. People who belong and who know they belong to Christ not only must "talk the talk" but "walk the walk," and evangelical education is about teaching the children of God to talk and walk with the mind of Christ.

EDUCATION FOR CRITICAL REFLECTION
(LIFE IN THE SPIRIT)

Evangelical education is not just for children and initiates newly baptized, however. Living into our baptism is a lifelong vocation for all of us in Christ. Older children, youth, and adults particularly will and must engage the gospel critically. They bring to the community's story and teachings doubts and challenges encountered in their "life in the Spirit" in a world not yet conformed to the mind of Christ.

Young children leave the relative security of knowing how things are done at home for the wider circle of school and friends from other household situations. They must learn how to communicate with and live and work beside those who offer genuine alternatives to our way of meaning. Understanding Christian faith and the life of faith must grow and expand along with these new experiences in order to provide meaning to disciples whose new questions require more adequate, complex, and nuanced responses from the church's traditions and witnesses.

As people grow, as their experiences multiply and their ability to see the world from other points of view develop, it is likely, even desirable, that they critically scrutinize what they have learned earlier about the church and the means of expressing their faith in Christ. What was once taken for granted in order to belong or feel a part of family and community is precisely what each person must test for its adequacy to provide meaning in the face of dramatic personal and social changes.

Rather than running from this challenge, evangelical education needs to embrace those whose critical skills and personal discomfort initially push against the community's shared memory and lifestyle in Christ. This embrace is also a witness to the faith community's confidence in the fullness and adequacy of the gospel to inform our constantly changing experiences of reality. Encouraging critical reflection in the community is, therefore, a way of proclaiming the gospel and renewing belief. Our beginning point is the conviction that the gospel is relevant in every generation and adequate to discerning the will of God in every circumstance.

It is commonplace to hear people talk about wanting "to make the Bible relevant" to our circumstances. But Reformed faith has no doubt of the Bible's relevance for any and all times, places, and peoples. The challenge for us is to have what Calvin called "a teachable spirit" so that we may hear the relevance of the gospel for our lives and let ourselves be transformed by the truth we see.

Evangelism and education join in this ongoing effort that all of us must make to interpret our new situations in the light of the gospel and to hear the gospel with self-consciousness and cultural-consciousness, open to the "new things" God is doing in our time. Youth need to see adult Christians constantly reforming their own beliefs, their ways of expressing the truth of the gospel, in the light of the world's needs.[13] Adults need to listen to and engage with youth in their efforts to bring sense and order to a chaotic adolescence in a fractured, frightening world.

Evangelical education attests to a courageous gospel and a courageous church, necessarily engaged in the dangerous work of living in the world but not of it. It calls for the risk of entertaining the ideas and claims of others in order to discern how God may be shaping God's word of reconciliation and hope in these days. It requires transforming the gospel's language of love into a contemporary vocabulary to communicate Christ again and again.

This is the prophetic work of evangelism, which calls the church back to its fundamental relationship with Christ, while urging the church forward toward a "promised land" where the word of God is done and justice and love live together in human community. In the faith community, we are prophet-evangelists to one another. We witness to the word of God we hear and see in the interaction between the biblical words we read and the contemporary experiences we must interpret. In this process, we are like the prophets. We remind one another of the disciples' covenant that binds us and pray for one another on the way to making faithful choices. That is what prophet-evangelists do, naming the distance between life as we know it and life as God wills it for us.

Classroom and small-group settings are appropriate for this prophetic task of evangelism, and the prophetic question that engages us is Micah's: "What does the Lord require of us?" More specifically, "How shall we do justice now, in Christ? How shall we show love mercifully now, in Christ? How shall we walk humbly now, with God in Christ?" This fundamental question finds particular form in a myriad of everyday questions about ordinary living faced by people. The evangelical teaching opportunity here is to gather folks to search for ways of responding to the questions of meaning and practice that contemporary life raises for Christians who are informed by both the deep, rich resources of the biblical witnesses and the traditions of the church and also mindful of the legitimate insights of the modern world.[14]

The implication of what I am suggesting is that we should rethink age segregation as a fundamental approach to determining all our educational structures. Congregations need to provide space and time for youth and adults of a variety of ages to struggle together to hear the gospel and to name their faithful responses to specific situations that challenge God's vision of justice and love for a new creation. The threat of addiction, manifest, for example, in drug and alcohol abuse and sexual promiscuity among youth, is not alone a youth problem; addictive behavior is cross-generational.

63

Its root causes lie in issues of fear and worth and dependency. The gospel of Christ has much to say, and finding solutions necessitates sharing the wisdom and witness of youth and adults together.

Confidence that the gospel is truly for our salvation can be found for youth and adults in their working together in congregations and at home so that they experience God's grace together in the context of a still broken world being healed in Christ. Further, this need for soul searching and experience sharing, for cooperative critical reflection on what we believe and what we have learned, in our search of God's presence and word for now, suggests educational settings and methods that maximize dialogue, self-expression, honest inquiry, and mutual support. As evangelists we know that Christ is repeatedly encountered "on the roads" disciples travel. As educators we need to make room for those experiences to be recounted when disciples come together "to break bread and to devote themselves to the apostles' teaching and to fellowship" (see Acts 2:42 and passim), so that the gospel may grow in the lives of growing Christians.

EDUCATION FOR PUBLIC TRANSFORMATION
(THE LIFE OF PUBLIC WITNESS)

Finally, a third task of evangelical education is to empower disciples for public witness. "Public witness" does not mean here teaching members to carry out denominational or nondenominational programs for evangelism, typically focused on church growth. Rather, it refers to relating the gospel of Christ to the public life and responsibilities of disciples who are also citizens of a particular city, state, province or nation.[15]

The position taken here assumes an evangelism that seeks to communicate the gospel's intention to establish a human community of justice and love by its willing and sometimes even dangerous participation in public dialogue in public space. In this arena, the common language is language of citizenship, rather than discipleship, and even where shared values do exist, they may or may not derive from a shared vision of Christ's new creation. The public concern of the church is the same as the gospel's concern: concern for the good of humankind and all creation. Historically, the church has contributed importantly to the public image of a common good, affirming, for example, the worth and value of human life; a vision of a peaceful, global community; and a celebration of the meaningfulness of ordinary work.

But how shall Christians express themselves for the common good in the public arena? The language of discipleship, which is the language of critical reflection and celebration within the community of faith, is not the language of citizenship. As citizens, for example, we have learned to talk prominently about personal rights and civil rights. These are concerns foreign to the biblical traditions, which claim no rights before God. As citizens, we owe allegiance to national purposes and locate our identities as citizens within the stories and symbols that make us Americans. But, as Christian citizens, our loyalty is first to God and God's universal purposes. We are formed, as we have seen, by the stories and symbols that make us Christians. Our public witness presents a communications problem. How shall we speak the love of God in Christ so that we may be understood in a public gathering of citizens, whose ordinary language is secular and whose values represent pluralistic commitments? How can we speak persuasively so that the unique image of God's justice and love that flows from the biblical witness to Christ can contribute to the search for social justice among diverse peoples at home and abroad?

If our challenge in the church educationally involves interpreting our experiences in the world in the light of the gospel, thereby reforming ourselves and the way we express that which we believe as Christians, then our challenge for educating for public ministry is nearly the reverse. To empower disciples for public witness requires articulating the gospel's vision and values in the language and behavior of public life. That is, disciples must be able to enter public debate about issues of justice, war, peace, health care, and human sexuality on terms that make sense in the marketplace of ideas that characterize our lives nationally and globally. But it is crucial that this be done without abandoning God's intentions for the good of all creation that we see revealed in scripture.

To pose our Christian responsibility as a choice between an agenda set by the church or an agenda set by the world is to set up a false dichotomy. The agenda of the church, if it is God's agenda, concerns the transformation of the world in the light of the promise that "God's will be done, on earth as it is in heaven." This transformation is ultimately the work of the Spirit and, therefore, presently the work of those who "walk in the Spirit." It is God's vision to fulfill; but it is our vision to walk by.

The disciples' witness in the public debate, therefore, is guided by the vision of God's coming rule, and it urges social structures and citizen behavior toward that goal. There is no pretense here to "build the realm of God." But the vision of God's concern for the healing and welfare of creation, for the care and shelter of the poor, and for full, meaningful, and purposeful human life dictates the public positions we may support and the social causes we may encourage. We can, indeed, help to build more just structures for human life, more hospitable structures for human relationships, and more life-renewing structures for caring for creation than currently characterize our national and international experience. Christian witness compels us to build now where we can in the image of God's commonwealth, and for that purpose, we need to educate evangelists for public witness.

This aspect of evangelism imagines church education for disciples whose citizenship is to be lived "in the Spirit."[16] Over the last half century at least, the church's once public voice has been muted in favor of church education devoted primarily to making good church members.[17] The task of evangelical education here is the recovery of a public voice for the church by helping members articulate the meaning of their faith for public policy and public decision making. Most of our daily lives is spent in the public domain: places of work, places of recreation, places of economic exchange. Evangelical education requires examining these spaces for gospel possibilities, for understanding what God may be doing in these places to redeem them, in order to join with God in that effort. Moreover, evangelical education for public witness means congregations making space and time in their buildings for opportunities to encourage and engage public discussion of issues, bringing together radically different, even competing voices within the sanctuary of the church's sponsorship.

Programs toward these goals are not hard to imagine, though they will not be easy to implement, given our own inexperience in public articulation of our faith. Thus debates concerning civil rights, community housing conditions, treatment of homeless persons, the desirability of political proposals, the place of homosexuals in the military, the use of public funds to support private schools, or the values taught in public-school education could constructively take place in local church buildings. Here Christian congregations can serve as peacemakers by providing opportunity for public discussion. It is risky business, since any genuine conversation opens all participants to change. But this is a risk the gospel requires of us.

CONCLUSION

The purpose of this volume of essays is to demonstrate that evangelism and being evangelical are concepts with deep roots in the Reformed heritage. Unfortunately, for multiple reasons discussed elsewhere in this collection, evangelism has, so to speak, fallen "among thieves" in the church, where it has been "beaten up and robbed" by an unfortunate constricting of its meaning to either a fundamentalist theology, a revivalist style of preaching, or a congregational campaign for new members. The loss is ours. Evangelical describes well Reformed theology and should fit comfortably the identity of contemporary Reformed Christians. It will do so, in fact, only when we find ways and means of talking about evangelism and of doing evangelizing that sustain our deep commitments to be ecumenical in our theology, responsible in our social witness, as well as open-minded and thorough in our educational efforts.

One of the hallmarks of Reformed faith of which Reformed Christians are appropriately proud is our historical emphasis on the importance of education. Calvin and the other Reformers recognized the indispensable need for an educated people of God—clergy and lay—if the priesthood of all believers and the commitment to the twin authority of *sola fides, sola gratia* was to be practiced by Christian believers. It never occurred to them that to be educated and to be evangelical needed to be contradictory aspirations. For this reason, this essay has offered one way to imagine this Reformed relationship between Christian education and evangelism. Evangelism, it has contended, is about disciple making, and so is church education.

Educational ministry that is evangelical in concern and style prepares the way for the gospel's encounter with children and adults in the three specific aspects of congregational life detailed above.

In all these tasks we need not start over. Pieces are in place everywhere. Our congregational life is readily adaptable to these evangelical and educational tasks. But we must consciously and intentionally reform what we are doing educationally, if we are to be faithful evangelists, responsive to our calling to "make disciples" of others and, not incidentally, of ourselves, by the grace of God's Holy Spirit.

NOTES

1. See Wayne Meeks, *The First Urban Christians: The Social World of the Apostle Paul* (New Haven, Conn.: Yale University Press, 1983), for a careful study of the social status of early converts to Christianity.

2. See, for example, Wade Clark Roof and William McKinney, *American Mainline Religion: Its Changing Shape and Future* (New Brunswick, N. J.: Rutgers University Press, 1987), 148–85.

3. On the complexities of the concept "conversion," see Beverly Roberts Gaventa, *From Darkness to Light: Aspects of Conversion in the New Testament* (Philadelphia: Fortress Press, 1986), who distinguishes helpfully between experiences usually incorporated in the idea of conversion. Changes that grow from previous experience but represent new role taking Gaventa calls alternation. Changes that reflect radical reorientation and new identity, accompanied by denial of one's past, she calls conversion; and those that are radical and offer new identity but without negating one's past, choosing instead to reinterpret the past in the light of new perception, Gaventa calls transformation. Conversion experiences within the Christian tradition, radical and dramatic though they may be, would tend toward transformation, typically; though under certain circumstances they may approximate the core of conversion.

4. On the evangelical origins and practices of the Sunday school movement, see especially Robert Lynn and Elliott Wright, *The Big Little School: 200 Years of the Sunday School* (Birmingham, Ala.: Religious Education Press, 1980).

5. Report of the Board of Christian Education, *Minutes of the General Assembly of the Presbyterian Church in the U.S.A.*, 1947, Part II, p. 87.

6. For a more extensive treatment of these developments, see David C. Hester, "The Use of the Bible in Presbyterian Curricula: 1923–1985," in *The*

Pluralistic Vision: Presbyterians and Mainstream Protestant Education and Leadership, ed. Milton J Coalter, John M. Mulder, Louis B. Weeks (Louisville, Ky.: Westminster/John Knox Press, 1992), 205–35.

7. The recognition that persons' lives and social situations have a text-like or narrative quality to them, which requires interpretation to understand their meaning, is shared by contemporary philosophers and theologians, including Paul Ricoeur, David Tracy, and Edward Farley. For specific insights concerning teaching and nonwritten texts, see Hunter McEwan, "Teaching and the Interpretation of Texts," *Educational Theory* 42 (winter 1992): 59–69.

8. See Walter Brueggemann, *The Creative Word: Canon as a Model for Biblical Education* (Philadelphia: Fortress Press, 1982), 1–45, for discussion of the meaning of "Torah" as the nonnegotiable knowledge necessary for community identity.

9. Deuteronomy 26:5–9 models such a retelling that transforms ancient liturgical story into present affirmation of belonging.

10. On meaning making as key to the process of human development, see the important work of Robert Kegan, *The Evolving Self: Problems and Process in Human Development* (Cambridge, Mass.: Harvard University Press, 1982).

11. For an excellent discussion of "life in the Spirit" in Reformed perspective related to educational ministry tasks, see the study paper from the Theology and Worship Unit, *Growing in the Life of Christian Faith* (Louisville, Ky.: Presbyterian Church (U.S.A.), 1989).

12. Ibid., 26–28.

13. See the excellent work of Sara Little, *To Set One's Heart: Belief and Teaching in the Church* (Atlanta: John Knox Press, 1983), 1–32, for the distinction between faith and belief. Little affirms, rightly, that reforming beliefs, not "enabling faith to grow," is the task of teaching.

14. This correlative method of practical theological decision making is clearly presented, among other places, in James D. Whitehead and Evelyn Eaton Whitehead, *Method in Ministry: Theological Reflection and Christian Ministry* (New York: Seabury Press, 1980).

15. We do not have space here for a necessarily lengthy discussion of the issues of church-state relationships or the several typologies suggested for understanding the mission of the church in secular culture. Familiar examples might include H. Richard Niebuhr's types in *Christ and Culture* (New York: Harper & Row, 1951) or those of Avery Dulles in *Models of the Church* (Garden City, N.Y.: Doubleday & Co., Inc., 1974) or those of David A. Roozen, William McKinney, and Jackson Carroll in *Varieties of Religious Presence: Mission in Public Life* (New York: Pilgrim Press, 1984). For contrast, see the "resident alien" argument of Stanley Hauerwas and William H. Willimon, *Resident Aliens* (Nashville: Abingdon Press, 1989). They argue for "witness by example" as the public mission of the church.

16. This complicated subject is well discussed in Mary Boys, ed., *Education for Citizenship and Discipleship* (New York: Pilgrim Press, 1988). See particularly the chapter "The Two Pedagogies: Discipleship and Citizenship," by John A. Coleman.

17. For a full discussion of this development, see Jack L. Seymour et al., *The Church in the Education of the Public: Refocusing the Task of Religious Education* (Nashville: Abingdon Press, 1984).

Part 2. Witness in the Reformed Past:
A Presbyterian Example

4. "Converted and Always Converting": Evangelism in the Early Reformed Tradition

CATHERINE GUNSALUS GONZÁLEZ

It is very clear that a missionary movement of the character that developed in the nineteenth century was not a significant part of the Reformed tradition in the sixteenth century or in the two centuries following. But it is also inaccurate to say that the tradition totally lacked a sense of mission. A different sort of evangelism was being carried out, and this prepared Reformed Christians theologically and psychologically for the great world mission thrust of the nineteenth century.

Why did it take several centuries for global mission to move to center stage in Reformed churches, and what actual mission projects and emphases developed during the period of the sixteenth and seventeenth centuries in particular? These are the questions of this essay.

It cannot be said that the sixteenth century was inhospitable to a missionary consciousness, since precisely at that time the Roman Catholic Church was engaged in one of the great missionary expansions in the history of the church. In his history of missions, Kenneth Scott Latourette gives several reasons for the lack of Protestant involvement. He points out that Spain and Portugal, both strongly Catholic, were involved in exploration, conquest, and the constant contact with new populations that such enterprises provided. Protestants, on the other hand, generally did not have such contacts until the following century. They did interact with the Turkish Muslims who were attempting to conquer Europe from the east. But such contact was not conducive to missions, except in rare cases like that of the Czech baron, Venceslaus Budovetz de Budov, who was a member of the *Unitas Fratrum,* allied with the Reformed tradition.

He was in Constantinople from 1577 to 1581 as part of the embassy from the Holy Roman Emperor Rudolf II. He tried to convert Muslims to his Protestant faith but evidently was successful with only one person. His theology was clearly Calvinist, and he corresponded with Theodore Beza in Geneva. He did not go to Turkey as a missionary, but finding himself there, he sought to be an effective lay witness to his faith.[1]

Even after Protestants began colonial empires in the seventeenth century, their work still differed from that of the Roman Catholics. The Spanish and Portuguese governments were concerned with missions, and therefore supported them. The governments of the major Protestant sea powers—England and the Netherlands—did not urge or demand efforts for the conversion of the populations they encountered or conquered, although individual Christians did make such efforts.[2] In addition, by the early seventeenth century, the papacy had taken over from civil governments the direction of new missions other than those under the direction of the Spanish and Portuguese. This added strength, central direction, and financing to Catholic missions. The Protestants had no such central planning or support.[3]

FACTORS INHIBITING
PROTESTANT MISSIONS

Clearly, Protestants in the sixteenth century were primarily concerned with the survival, organization, and expansion of their churches over against the Catholic in Europe and Britain. This would be a serious issue until the close of the religious wars in the mid-seventeenth century. The Catholic Iberian Peninsula was not a battlefield in these wars and therefore could turn its attention outward.

Latourette points out that by rejecting the monastic vocation, Protestants also eliminated the major structure that, historically, had carried out Catholic missions. It would be some time before Protestants developed new models of missionary activity.[4]

The writings of the sixteenth-century leaders of the Reformed tradition reveal two other reasons—theological in character—that limited the vision of mission outside the area already dominated by the church. First, the Reformed tradition held a very positive view of the state. The civil government was a gift from God, and part of its task was to guard and support the church. However much Huldreich Zwingli and John Calvin might differ on the exact relation of church and state, both of them and their followers assumed that the state had many responsibilities in regard to the church. This did not mean a passive subservience to the state. Indeed, John Knox could call upon all citizens, not just powerful ones, to reform the church in which they lived, and to demand such reform from their political leaders.[5] However, the thought of a church being planted in a situation where the state had no concern for it, or was even hostile to it, was not a part of the Reformers' thinking. When the state expanded its power geographically into areas in which the church did not already exist, then they could imagine a mission there.[6] Protestant governments began such expansions in the period following the defeat of the Spanish Armada in 1588. Before that, there was little reason for a sense of world mission.

Second, the role and authority of bishops in general and the bishop of Rome in particular was obviously a major issue for Protestants. Calvin addressed this clearly in the *Institutes of the Christian Religion,* 4.3.4. Because this section is foundational to much of the Reformed tradition's understanding of offices in the church, it must be quoted at length:

> Apostles . . . were sent out to lead the world back from rebellion to true obedience to God, and to establish his Kingdom everywhere by the preaching of the gospel, or, if you prefer, as the first builders of the church, to lay its foundations in all the world.
>
> Paul applies the name "prophets" not to all those who were interpreters of God's will, but to those who excelled in a particular revelation. This class either does not exist today or is less commonly seen.
>
> "Evangelists" I take to be those who, although lower in rank than apostles, were next to them in office and functioned in their place. Such were Luke, Timothy, Titus, and others like them; perhaps also the seventy disciples, whom Christ appointed in the second place after the apostles.
>
> According to this interpretation (which seems to me to be in agreement with both the words and opinion of Paul), these three functions were not established in the church as permanent

75

ones, but only for that time during which churches were to be erected where none existed before, or where they were to be carried over from Moses to Christ. Still, I do not deny that the Lord has sometimes at a later period raised up apostles, or at least evangelists in their place, as has happened in our own day. For there was need for such persons to lead the church back from the rebellion of Antichrist. Nonetheless, I call this office "extraordinary," because in duly constituted churches it has no place.

The argument continues into section 5:

Next come pastors and teachers, whom the church can never go without. . . . For as our teachers correspond to the ancient prophets, so do our pastors to the apostles.

and in section 6:

Finally, what the apostles performed for the whole world, each pastor ought to perform for his own flock, to which he is assigned.[7]

The concern in these sections of the *Institutes* was the doctrine of apostolic succession in the Roman Catholic Church, which gave the bishops an authority that Calvin did not accept.

For Calvin, the apostles were a temporary office in the early church. Together with their subordinates, the evangelists, they planted the churches. Now that task has been done, except for extraordinary circumstances. Calvin found the Reformation itself such an extraordinary time, and evidently Martin Luther was in his mind when he wrote that such an extraordinary office had been raised up in his own day to call the church back to faithfulness. But the true successors of the apostles are the pastors of congregations. That is the permanent office that parallels the office of apostle in the early church. A bishop is a pastor and a pastor is a bishop.

Such an argument was helpful against the authority of bishops. It denied that there was a form of apostolic succession that devolved on the episcopal office rather than on pastors. Essentially, Calvin denied that there was any continuing office established by Christ that was superior to the pastor. The centrality of preaching also led to an emphasis on the pastoral role since Catholic bishops did not preach.

However, it did leave open the question of how new congregations could be established in places where there were no churches.

The only occasion where Calvin addressed such a question was when he supported the efforts of a group of French Huguenots to establish a church in Brazil. The settlement was to provide a place for French Protestants to worship without fear of persecution and to offer a mission to the neighboring Tupinamba Indians.[8] In this situation, the group included two pastors. A congregation was being created in Europe and transplanted, with the task of evangelizing their new neighbors. From letters sent back, the method employed for mission was for the Europeans to witness to the natives by their own lives, but they also commissioned the adolescent men in the European group to learn the native language by living among the Indians, so that they could later preach the gospel to them. Conflicts soon arose in the group, especially when the civil leader attempted to impose Catholic practices on the church. The Protestants eventually returned to Europe, except for those who were killed by the civil administrator, and the colony was ended by the Portuguese. It had had a brief life of about two years, from 1556 to 1558.[9]

This belief that the continuity of the apostolic office and its secondary form of evangelists was now lodged in the pastoral office continued into the next generations of Reformed theologians. In the 1626 *Compendium Theologiae Christianae* by Johannes Wallebius of Basel, the author divided ministers into two categories: extraordinary and ordinary. He wrote:

> The extraordinary ones are those men who God raises up either for establishing a new regime in the church, or for restoring the old when it had broken down.
> Such, under the Old Testament, were the prophets. In the time of the New Testament, John the Baptist, Christ, the apostles, the prophets (i.e., men with the gift of interpreting Scripture), the evangelists.[10]

Because evangelists held an extraordinary, not ordinary, office in the church, a strong state church system would divide the entire area of the state into parishes. There was no place without an assigned pastor. The pastor was concerned that all residents in the area should be faithful worshipers, but there were no other church officers that could come in from outside the parish to evangelize, except at times when the whole church had fallen away and needed to be revitalized. The Protestant Reformation was clearly such a period. But once the Reformation had occurred, there was no further need for evangelists.

Two points are significant here. First, the Reformed tradition developed a model for mission that included the transplanting of congregations with their pastors. This made sense in a period of colonization when lay people were willing to become permanent residents in colonies. The abortive colony in Brazil already mentioned was such an instance. More long-lasting were the early New England colonies, and even some of the later internal migration westward within the English colonies. But this model also points to the dominance of the pastoral role within Reformed thinking. A minister without a congregation was almost unimaginable. This would severely limit the possibility of missionaries traveling into new areas without an accompanying congregation. Struggle with this theological inheritance would later develop in Reformed history.

PROTESTANT MISSIONARY ZEAL

Protestant evangelistic zeal and a sense of mission did exist. In his commentary on Isaiah 12:4–5, Calvin wrote:

> Hence it is evident what is the desire which ought to be cherished among all the godly. It is, that the goodness of God may be *made known* to all, that all may join in the same worship of God. We ought especially to be inflamed with this desire, after having been delivered from some alarming danger, and most of all after having been delivered from the tyranny of the devil and from everlasting death. . . . It is our duty to proclaim the goodness of God to every nation.[11]

However, this duty of proclaiming to every nation had to wait until the Reformers had proclaimed the gospel to those who, though baptized, were seen to have little or no real faith, as understood by Protestants. Early Reformers directed their evangelistic work almost exclusively to "converting" Roman Catholics in Europe to the Protestant persuasion.

Ecumenical Protestants may not care for the term "conversion" being used for those who change from one denomination to another. They may particularly oppose the term in regard to a change from Roman Catholic to Protestant, as though a Catholic is not Christian. Others use the term easily to mean any transformation to a lively faith, whether from no faith at all or from lukewarm participation in any Christian church, even if there is no change in denomination. However, the sixteenth-century Reformers generally meant by conversion the experience of faith as Protestants understood it, and, therefore, they readily used it for the change from participation in the Roman Catholic Church to becoming a convinced member of a Protestant church.

Early Protestant understandings of mission were then a matter of expanding the circles of evangelism, from those closest at hand in Europe to those outside the traditionally Christian world when they happened to become the geographic neighbors of colonizing Protestants. Only after these seedbeds of colonization were well under way would Protestants expand their evangelism to the larger non-Christian world. If this understanding is correct, then it is fair to say that Protestants were involved in mission in these early centuries, but their missionary thrust was toward their nominal Christian neighbors in Europe.

A few Reformers specifically opposed the expansion of the church beyond the borders of the then-Christian world. One of the most glaring examples was Zacharias Ursinus, one of the authors of the Heidelberg Catechism. Ursinus was convinced that pagans were savages, unable to tolerate strangers who might preach to them, and persecutors of the Christian faith. Therefore, holy things ought not be given to such dogs.[12]

THE EXPANSION OF PROTESTANT MISSIONS

By the end of the sixteenth and the beginning of the seventeenth century, at least two Protestant countries were involved in colonial expansion: the Netherlands and England. Home churches in these countries were concerned about their responsibility for evangelism in their new colonies. The native people needed to hear the message of salvation, but the Dutch and English churches did not clearly state that these populations would be damned if they did not hear and respond to it.

The Netherlands

In 1590, a Dutch pastor, Adrianus Savaria, insisted that there was a clear duty to preach the gospel to all creatures, and this duty was binding on all Christians.[13] Seminary professors as well as pastors became increasingly concerned about missions.[14] In 1595, the Dutch Calvinists sent missions to the East Indies and Ceylon and translated the Bible into Malay.[15] In 1618, Justus van Heurn in Leiden requested missions to the East Indies, and in 1622 a seminary for training missionaries was established in Leiden. During the next ten years, twelve men were sent.[16]

The commercial expansion of the Dutch altered the view of mission in the Netherlands. Even if one had been absorbed in the task of reforming and transforming the faith of those who had been lackluster members of the church, an evangelical spirit cannot simply be turned off because the people one encounters have never heard the gospel. It was now changed into the task of world mission. State support was present at least to some degree with the colonial enterprise itself.

However, there were clear limitations to missions in the Netherlands. The East India Company, in charge of the eastward commercial expansion, did not want such missions, and in fact, strongly opposed them. Within the Dutch church there were voices in support of missions, and some missions efforts were even attempted, but the voices remained isolated, and they did not presage official church support for such work. Nor did the church use the influence at its command to encourage the civil government to support such activities.[17]

Great Britain

An account of evangelism from England, in contrast, is complicated by two particular problems. First, the division between

European and American history is obviously murky since the colonial connection across the Atlantic was very strong in the seventeenth century. Therefore, mission activities of the British in the American colonies must be a part of this history.

Second, exactly which British church groups need to be considered is not obvious. "Puritan" is an unclear term in the seventeenth century, since it incorporates participants from a variety of denominations. Furthermore, Puritans and Dutch Calvinists can both be classified as part of the Scholastic or Orthodox movement, with good reason. As such, they are usually contrasted with the Pietist movement, stemming largely from German Lutheranism, which had a strong concern for the experience of faith but less interest in precise doctrine than did the Orthodox. This contrast between Orthodoxy and Pietism makes some sense when one is concerned with the specific issue of precise, logical doctrinal statements, but with regard to an evangelical concern for missions it is not at all helpful. In fact, such a contrast overlooks some very significant interconnections and parallels between German Pietism and English Puritanism, both in the Old World and in the colonies.

It might be better to see both Puritanism and Pietism as part of a single movement of renewed concern for the devout religious life of Christians as it is lived out in the world. The Puritan stress on sanctification added a dimension beyond the intellectual pursuit of proper doctrine. Religious experience could therefore find a place among Reformed Scholastics. This was in contrast to the Lutheran Scholastics for whom precise doctrinal formulation was the dominant concern. The split between Orthodox and Pietists was therefore greater on the Lutheran side, whereas Puritans had strong marks of both groups without apparent conflict.[18]

THE PURITANS AND MISSIONS

Richard Sibbes was born in 1577, and though a Puritan, he remained within the Church of England all his life. He was clear that a person's salvation is totally due to the action of God, but he was also convinced that God required the church to proclaim the gospel and God's requirement to repent and believe. This duty to proclaim the gospel was incumbent on the whole church, laity and clergy alike. Wherever we are, we are to witness to our neighbors.[19]

Sibbes did not recognize a particular church vocation of missionary, but he did believe that all Christians, wherever they were, were to be missionaries as part of their life of faith. No distinction was necessary, then, between Christians in England who called their not so faithful neighbors to a sincere discipleship, and Christians from England who traveled abroad to areas where the gospel had never been proclaimed. The same duty was laid upon all. However, Sibbes did acknowledge that there were new opportunities because merchants and sailors in his day were going to unevangelized locales. He therefore urged those who found themselves in such places to carry the gospel to all whom they met. Indeed, Sibbes suggested a missiological interpretation of the parable of the talents. According to Sibbes, the gospel has been entrusted to us even as the master gave coins to his servants. We are not to bury the gospel in the ground by keeping it to ourselves with no increase in the number of faithful. Instead, we are to spend it on others by sharing the gospel, thereby reaping an increase in those who glorify God. Clearly, God is the cause of others coming to faith. It is not our work. But God seeks to use the ordinary means of the gospel's proclamation to accomplish this, and all Christians are part of that ordinary means of proclamation[20]

A second major early Puritan thinker who dealt with missions was Richard Baxter, born in 1615. Baxter specifically took issue with the idea that the office of evangelist and apostolic work were only temporary and did not continue beyond the early church. The gifts and calling to the task of spreading the gospel to those who have not heard it did indeed continue, since the gospel has not been proclaimed to the whole world.[21]

Baxter agreed with Sibbes that all Christians are called to bear witness to their neighbors, but he made provision for some special calling with this regard. He was particularly concerned for the translation of Bibles and other Christian materials into the languages of those to whom the gospel had not yet been proclaimed. He wrote: "It is not only lawful, but one of the best works in the world, for fit persons to go on a design to convert the poor infidels and heathens where they go. Therefore the preachers of the gospel should not be backward to take any opportunity, as chaplains to ambassadors, or in factories [colonial trading posts], etc., to put themselves in such a way."[22]

The intentionality with which this mission is planned is an advance beyond the thinking of Sibbes. In fact, Baxter makes room for an "unfixed minister" who is able to carry out evangelism without having a congregation as his base.[23]

Baxter also was aware that the great division of the churches made mission difficult. Therefore, he pointed to the need for unity if mission is to be successful. He blamed the Roman Catholic Church for the division that had occurred.[24] He also challenged the notion that a supportive civil government must exist before missions can be undertaken. In the early church, Christians clearly sought to evangelize others, even though the state opposed their mission. Moreover, the words of Christ in Matthew 28 are "to preach & disciple & baptize all nations, without excepting those whose lawes forbad it."[25]

The thinking of Richard Baxter had been pushed forward on the topic of mission by some very concrete examples, and he became a leader in the concern for mission that was growing in the British Reformed churches of his time. It is at this point that the connection between the British at home and those in the American colonies cannot be overlooked.

John Eliot left England for New England in 1631 at the age of twenty-seven. As a Puritan minister, he went to Boston to preach. He was there only a year, and then settled in nearby Roxbury, where he lived until his death in 1690. A positive relationship existed between the colonists and the native Narragansetts. Influenced by Sibbes and other Puritan leaders, Eliot assumed himself duty bound to proclaim the gospel to these new neighbors.[26] He remained the pastor of an English congregation, even though Baxter had argued that unfixed ministers were possible and necessary for mission work. Baxter had direct contact with Eliot through letters. He was involved in support for the Corporation for the Propagation of the Gospel in New England, an organization that published tracts written in New England describing the mission work with the Indians. At the time of the founding of this supportive society in 1649, almost twelve thousand pounds were raised. Tracts published by the society were also sold for the purpose of raising money to support the missions, and printed reports of Eliot's work in the colonies directly fostered growing interest in missions among Christians in England.[27] In addition to tracts, letters from those engaged in mission were copied and shared widely, and these proved to be important means by which the idea of the church's missionary task was spread.

Baxter's stress on the evangelization of neighbors who had never heard the gospel led him to turn to the question of evangelizing slaves. Many slaveholders opposed such missions on the grounds that Christian slaves might need to be freed. Baxter found their attitude an impediment to mission and therefore contrary to the gospel. He became quite opposed to slavery.[28]

Knowledge of Eliot's work among the Indians also spread to the Netherlands. There it raised the Reformed churches' interest in developing similar work in the East Indies.[29] Within Puritanism, even where concern for evangelization existed, there was great hesitation to allow ministers who were not also pastors of congregations to carry on such mission. In time this also would be overcome.

The writings of Baxter were preparing the groundwork for this. It was obvious to Baxter that the task of mission was greatly complicated by the division of languages. He wrote:

> No part of my Prayers are so deeply serious, as that for the Conversion of the Infidel and Ungodly World, that God's Name may be sanctified, and his Kingdom come, and his Will be done on Earth as it is in Heaven: Nor was I ever before so sensible what a Plague the Division of Languages was which hindereth our speaking for their Conversion; nor what a *great Sin tyranny* is, which keepeth out the Gospel from most of the Nations of the World.[30]

Baxter had specific ideas for overcoming this difficulty of translating the gospel message into another culture and language. He recognized that this required great preparation and skill. He wanted those with money to support a school for training those who were able and willing to dedicate their lives to learning the necessary languages and then going out as missionaries. He also urged Christians involved in colonial enterprises to take such missionaries on their journeys and support their work in colonial areas. He arranged to have a wealthy Puritan fund the translation of Hugo Grotius's *De*

Veritate Religionis Christianae into Arabic. This was done in 1660, and he urged the Dutch East India Company to distribute the book in the areas of their colonization.[31]

For Baxter, the Jesuits had provided an excellent example of what could be done. Perhaps as part of the ecumenical spirit that is to be found in much of his writings, Baxter specifically opposed those Protestants who condemned the work of the Jesuits and yet did nothing themselves toward the evangelization of non-Christians. He wrote:

> I take it to be my duty *greatly to honour them,* for what they have done in Congo, Japan, China & other countries. . . . I thinke them much more laudable that did those great things though in a culpable manner, than those Protestants that ever had opportunity, & have done nothing themselves, but find fault with them that did it.[32]

He read with great interest the work of the Spanish Jesuit, Joseph Acosta, *The Natural and Moral History of the Indians.*[33]

On the other hand, John Eliot saw little if any good in the work of the Jesuits. In fact, he believed their missions to be the work of the Antichrist. He particularly objected to the Jesuits' practice of adopting some of the native culture and customs into Christian worship. Eliot maintained that only "a *pure, plain Scripture worship* would do."[34]

PIETISM AND PURITANISM

As mentioned earlier, the usual division between German Pietism and Puritanism overlooks the considerable connection between the two, and therefore hides the Reformed concern for mission. These connections existed in three dimensions: (1) the influence of English Puritans on Dutch Pietism and, through that, the influence on German Pietism; (2) the significance of Pietism in the Netherlands and the rise of the evangelical spirit in Dutch Reformed churches in the American colonies; and (3) the correspondence between Cotton Mather and August Francke concerning mission.

Politically and theologically there were strong connections between England and Holland during the seventeenth century. The royal families were linked in a way that would lead to the ascension of William and Mary to the throne of England in the Glorious Revolution. But even earlier, before the Commonwealth, when the Puritans were out of favor in England, some found refuge with the Dutch. In 1610, the English theologian William Ames settled in the Netherlands. In his book *The Marrow of Theology*, he placed great stress on the work of the Holy Spirit in the Christian life, and therefore on the experiential side of the religious life. Ames had a powerful influence on those in the Dutch church who were concerned about the life of piety. He also served as a consultant for the Synod of Dort, showing the compatibility, at least for some, of an emphasis on religious experience along with concern for orthodox doctrine.[35] In addition to Ames's work, several major writings of English Puritans, particularly those concerned with the life of piety, were translated into Dutch.

Many Dutch theologians also studied in England. One of the major Dutch pietists, William Teellinck (1579–1629), had studied in England and had married an Englishwoman. He maintained his contact with the Puritans over the years.[36]

The pietist movement within the Dutch church was concerned for holiness of life and also for the evangelical character of experienced grace. In its early development Pietism had been influenced by the former Jesuit Jean de Labadie, who had joined the Reformed movement and had been in France and Geneva before coming to the Netherlands. Labadie strongly emphasized the work of the Holy Spirit, and he established small groups of those who were committed to this new life in the Spirit. Eventually the groups he organized in the Netherlands separated from the Dutch Reformed Church. Major Dutch pietists opposed this action, but the Dutch pietists nevertheless retained the use of small groups for prayer and Bible study. They were concerned about evangelism.[37] Two members of the separatist Labadist group came to the American colonies in 1679 to visit associated groups in Maryland and Delaware. In the following year they traveled to Boston and there met with John Eliot. They were most impressed with his work among the Indians. They wrote that he was "the best of the ministers whom we have yet heard."[38]

The stress on evangelism that led the Dutch churches to support missions in the East Indies also spread to the Dutch Reformed groups in the English colonies. James Tanis argues persuasively that the dominant influence on Theodore Frelinghuysen was this vibrant Reformed Pietism of the Netherlands rather than Pietism's German Lutheran forms.[39] The same can be said of the influences on the eighteenth-century Presbyterian revivalist Gilbert Tennent.[40] The significance of these two figures for the Evangelical Revival in the American colonies during the 1730s and 1740s cannot be overstated.

But even more interesting is the documented relationship between major figures in the American revivals and the German pietists who were concerned for mission. In 1705, the king of Denmark turned to August Francke in Halle for trained missionaries to send to the East Indian colony of Tranquebar.[41] At the time, Francke knew nothing of any missions among the Indians in New England. However, through correspondence with Cotton Mather, Francke later received Mather's written survey of the Protestant work among the Native Americans in New England, in which Mather expressed his own understanding of missions. In turn, Francke sent Mather word about the work of the missionaries sent to Tranquebar and other locations in the East Indies. Francke wrote:

> Providence hath cast Your Lot in *America,* a Country abounding with numerous and barbarous Nations, who living without the Pales of the Christian Church, stand in need as much as those in the *East,* of the saving Light of the Gospel. I do not doubt, but it would be very agreeable to our Missionaries, if a Letter from your Hand did give 'em a full Account of all such *Methods* as hitherto have been made use of for converting your *West-India* Heathens to the Christian Faith.[42]

Ultimately, Mather began corresponding directly with the Halle missionaries in Tranquebar.

Mather was well aware of the Catholic missions in North America, and he agreed with Eliot that such missions are the work of the Antichrist. He urged Protestants to be much more concerned for their own mission work. Yet Mather was quite ecumenical in his stress on the need for unity among Protestants in mission, since mission requires the central doctrines be stressed rather than the less essential ones on which Christians disagree. For Mather, the essential doctrines were the Trinity, the incarnation and work of Christ, and the Christian life, which consists of loving God and our neighbor.[43]

Whereas some European theologians could consider that the work of proclaiming the gospel "to the ends of the earth" was a task already completed by the early apostles, the colonists whose neighbors were Native Americans had great difficulty with such an opinion. "The ends of the earth" for the apostolic age did not include the New World, so some new thinking about the task of carrying the gospel to those who had not heard it obviously needed to be done. In fact, Mather believed that with the proclamation of the gospel to the real "ends of the earth" the final age of the Holy Spirit was beginning.[44]

Ernst Benz concludes his study of the correspondence between Mather and Francke with these words:

> It is not just a phrase when Cotton Mather calls the Puritanism of New England and its particular spiritual tendency the "Pietism of this place" and "the American Pietism." There is, indeed, a deep inner harmony in the fundamental view of the nature of Christianity between Pietism and Puritanism. In truth, there are only differences of style between the two movements: German Pietism shows a stronger mystical influence, whereas American Puritanism shows a stronger ethical emphasis and with its Calvinistic heritage stresses election and predestination more. In the individual personalities these differences are almost completely eliminated. Francke thought Cotton Mather was a Pietist after his own fashion; whereas Cotton Mather considered his friend from Halle who worked energetically in the field of social ethics to be a true Puritan.[45]

It would appear that a stress on the work of the Spirit that leads to a renewed Christian life for those who have grown up within the church leads also to a desire to share this experience of renewal with others in the church. Such evangelism cannot be stopped at the borders of the existing church. When historical circumstances make these Christians aware of others who have not heard the gospel, the desire to bring them the good news leads inexorably to missions.

The Puritans and the Pietists—those whose experience of renewal came within Calvinism or Lutheranism—were part of a common movement, and influences went back and forth across national and confessional boundaries.

Nor did this interconnection cease in the seventeenth century. Jonathan Edwards edited and published the journal of David Brainerd, one of the later missionaries to the Native Americans in New England. This book had significant influence in Great Britain, as did many of the writings of Edwards. In fact, it was these writings that strongly influenced William Carey at the beginning of the fully developed missionary movement of the nineteenth century.[46]

The connections between Puritanism and Pietism continued in John Wesley. His mother was strongly impressed by the accounts of the missionaries in Tranquebar, and she supported John's work in Georgia among the Indians.[47] John himself later urged all ministers to read Edwards's *Life of David Brainerd.*[48]

Wesley had arguments both with the Moravian Pietists on some issues and with the English Puritans on others. But their common agreement on the experienced reality of renewal through the action of the Holy Spirit and the consequent emphasis on missions was a common heritage from both sources. In neither the seventeenth nor the eighteenth century is it possible to divide the movements of Pietism and Puritanism into separate groups. The influence of both of these movements in Europe continued in the churches of the American colonies.

CONCLUSION

In summary, there was a clear evangelical thrust in the Reformed tradition from its inception in the sixteenth century. At first, the stress on the local congregation as the basic context for ordained ministry limited the deployment of missionaries. However, even with such a limitation, there was the increasing assumption that all Christians, not only the ordained, were witnesses of their faith to all their neighbors—whether Roman Catholic, nominal Protestant, or totally unacquainted with Christianity—with the hope of bringing them also to a lively faith. As colonial migrations changed the neighbors, the circle of mission increased. Faith was understood to be an experienced reality, and the experience was conversion, whatever the church affiliation or lack of it before such an experience. The church "Reformed and always reforming" was also the church "converted and always converting."

NOTES

1. Josef Soucek, "Venceslaus Budovetz de Budov (First Protestant Missionary to the Mohammedans)," *The Moslem World* 17 (1927): 401–3; and Samuel M. Zwemer, "Calvinism and the Missionary Enterprise," *Theology Today* 7 (1950): 215.

2. Kenneth Scott Latourette, *A History of the Expansion of Christianity* (New York: Harper & Brothers, 1939), 3:25–26.

3. Ibid., 33–35.

4. Ibid., 25–26.

5. John Knox, "Letter to the Commonalty of Scotland," in *The Political Writings of John Knox,* ed. Marvin A. Breslow (Washington, D.C.: Folger Shakespeare Library, 1985), 153–54.

6. Johannes van den Berg, *Constrained by Jesus' Love* (Kampen: J. H. Kok, 1956), 14.

7. *Calvin: Institutes of the Christian Religion,* ed. John T. McNeill, trans. Ford Lewis Battles, The Library of Christian Classics, vols. 20 and 21 (Philadelphia: Westminster Press, 1960), 4.3.4–6.

8. G. Baez-Camargo, "The Earliest Protestant Missionary Venture in Latin America," *Church History* 21 (1952): 135.

9. Ibid., 140–43.

10. Johannes Wallebius, quoted in *Reformed Dogmatics,* ed. John W. Beardslee III (New York: Oxford University Press, 1965), 142.

11. John Calvin, *Commentary on the Book of the Prophet Isaiah,* trans. William Pringle (Grand Rapids: Baker Book House, 1979), 1:403.

12. Justo L. González, *Historia de las misiones* (Buenos Aires: La Aurora, 1970), 188–89.

13. Latourette, *Expansion,* 3:43.

14. van den Berg, *Constrained,* 19.

15. Zwemer, "Missionary Enterprise," 212.

16. Latourette, *Expansion,* 3:43.

17. van den Berg, *Constrained,* 21.

18. F. Ernest Stoeffler, *German Pietism during the Eighteenth Century* (Leiden: E. J. Brill, 1973), 218; Milton J Coalter, *Gilbert Tennent, Son of Thunder* (New York: Greenwood Press, 1986), xix.

19. Sidney H. Rooy, *The Theology of Missions in the Puritan Tradition* (Grand Rapids: Wm. B. Eerdmans Publishing Co., 1965), 31, 42.

20. Ibid., 63–64.

21. Ibid., 100.

22. Richard Baxter, quoted in ibid., 111.

23. Ibid., 150.

24. Ibid., 112–13.

25. Quoted in ibid., 125–26.

26. Ibid., 156–57.

27. Ibid., 63, 160; van den Berg, *Constrained,* 25.

28. Rooy, *Missions,* 134, 159.

29. van den Berg, *Constrained,* 25.

30. Rooy, *Missions,* 132–33.

31. Ibid., 110–11, 69.

32. Ibid., 126.

33. Ibid., 129.

34. Ibid., 226, 275.

35. William Ames, *The Marrow of Theology,* ed. and trans. John D. Eusden (Boston: Pilgrim Press, 1968), 36.

36. F. Ernest Stoeffler, *Continental Pietism and Early American Christianity* (Grand Rapids: Wm. B. Eerdmans Publishing Co., 1976), 34–35; Coalter, *Tennent,* xix.

37. James Tanis, *Dutch Calvinistic Pietism in the Middle Colonies: A Study in the Life and Theology of Theodorus Jacobus Frelinghuysen* (The Hague: Martinus Nijhoff, 1967), 20–22; James Tanis, "Reformed Pietism in Colonial America," in Stoeffler, *Continental Pietism,* 41; Rooy, *Missions,* 320–21.

38. Rooy, *Missions,* 159; Perry Miller and Thomas H. Johnson, *The Puritans,* rev. ed. (New York: Harper & Row, 1963), 403.

39. Tanis, *Dutch Calvinistic Pietism,* 1–2.

40. Coalter, *Tennent,* xix.

41. Stoeffler, *German Pietism,* 35.

42. Ernst Benz, "Pietist and Puritan Sources of Early Protestant World Missions," trans. Luise Jockers, *Church History* 20 (June 1951): 38.

43. Ibid., 43–45.

44. Ibid., 48–49.

45. Ibid., 51.

46. van den Berg, *Constrained,* 25.

47. Ibid., 87–88.

48. Robert C. Monk, *John Wesley: His Puritan Heritage* (Nashville: Abingdon Press, 1966), 221.

5. Awakenings to New Possibilities in Outreach: Evangelism in Pre–Civil War American Presbyterianism

EDITH L. BLUMHOFER

Evangelism is an integral part of the story of American Christianity. Its influence has been so pervasive that even the groups that seem least enamored of evangelism have been shaped in part by their encounter with it. Periodic revivals have often motivated people to evangelism, and those denominations that most readily accommodated the evangelistic impulse experienced rapid growth in the early republic.

American Christianity has also often manifested a related, powerful impulse to restorationism. From the seventeenth-century Puritans, who determined that primitive Christianity would flourish in the New World, to the twentieth-century Pentecostals, who regarded their religious experience as the restoration of "the faith once delivered to the saints," many American Christians have worked to realize an elusive spiritual dynamic they associate with New Testament times. In the past, restorationism has often been associated with revivals and with specific groups—the Disciples of Christ, the Church of Jesus Christ of Latter-day Saints, the Pentecostals. In the contemporary setting, when restorationism and evangelism are the topics of discussion, Presbyterians are hardly the first to come to mind.

At first reading, then, it is surprising to find Samuel Miller, professor of ecclesiastical history and church government at Princeton Theological Seminary, arguing eloquently in 1842 that Presbyterianism incarnated "the truly primitive and apostolic constitution of the church of Christ." Miller supported this claim with various New Testament precedents for the tradition's principal doctrinal stances. He managed to conclude his argument without broaching one basic ingredient of the New Testament church in action, however: he neglected evangelism—a curious omission, given the prominence of evangelism in the New Testament model.[1] Yet perhaps it was not so curious, at least if revivalists' unrelenting critiques of Presbyterian Calvinism had any validity.[2]

The Presbyterian story affords an instructive case study in how American churches have adapted to new social and cultural situations. Sometimes adaptation has proceeded easily; at other times resistance to adaptation has been a major story line. In a culture dedicated to religious freedom and democracy as well as captivated by the possibilities it offered "self-made" men and women, Presbyterians wrestled with the relationship between divine initiative and the human will, between reason and faith, piety and intellect.

The revivals of the early nineteenth century and their most prominent proponent, Charles Finney, focused the tensions evangelism awakened for Presbyterians. Presbyterians might have prided themselves on proper form and constitution, but they could not seem to agree about the patterns of religious experience revivalistic Protestants generally associated with evangelism. Presbyterians had in common their devotion to the Westminster Standards, but that devotion did not shape a common approach to the soul winning that fueled spectacular growth among Baptists and Methodists. Mark Twain's many readers have smiled knowingly for a century when reading Huck Finn's observations on how capably mid-nineteenth-century Presbyterians could hold forth at the Sunday dinner table on the fine points of Reformed theology. This pastime was applauded and cultivated by seminarians such as Miller, although it helped account for the way Baptist and Methodist numbers surpassed Presbyterian membership counts.

Presbyterian leaders were reluctant at times to acknowledge the strength of another strand in their tradition, a strand perhaps more accurately representing the experience of the people in the pew than did the pronouncements of the denomination's acknowledged leaders. Side by side with the emphasis on intellect and order stood a venerable tradition of piety that drank deeply at the wells of American revivalism. It resonated with familiar themes: individual souls needed salvation; and the fate of America and of the world hung on the Christian response to that fact. Advocates of this evangelical approach maintained that simple gospel preaching and rigorous moral teaching promised God's spiritual and temporal favor.[3] The style and content of the revival message often seemed at odds, however, with the intellectual integrity Presbyterian leaders cherished. By mid-century when Miller wrote and Finney taught (by this time, the era's best-known evangelist had turned Oberlin professor), the issues had a long and divisive history. To understand the Presbyterian dilemma about evangelism as the United States faced the Civil War, one must look back to Presbyterian beginnings in colonial America. Like all other transplanted institutions, the Presbyterian Church faced new challenges to both its assumptions and its workings when it arrived in the colonies.

THE NEW WORLD SITUATION

As spiritual heirs of John Calvin, colonial Presbyterians had much in common with the Puritans who dominated early New England Protestantism. Presbyterians were scattered among the colonies from the 1640s, but Francis Makemie, an ordained Scotch-Irish missionary to America, first gathered them in the Middle Colonies after his arrival from Ireland in 1683. An itinerant missionary in North Carolina, Maryland, New York, Virginia, and New England, Makemie and six other ministers formed the Presbytery of Philadelphia in 1706. Within a decade, the organization had mushroomed and a synod had been formed with four constituent presbyteries, twenty-five ministers, and some three thousand members.[4]

Makemie's tireless missionary efforts were directed as much toward rounding up the baptized as toward churching the unchurched, and they illustrate the contrast between the situation in the Old World and the New. Many American Presbyterians were of Scotch-Irish stock; others were English, while strong Presbyterian influences molded Reformed communities of continental European immigrants as well. Their religious tradition had been formed and tested in a cultural setting that diverged sharply from the situation in the New World.

In the Old World, every square foot of ground was part of some parish; churches dotted the landscape; evangelism was as much a matter of the cultivation of piety as of the persuasion of the unchurched. Baptized people needed to be awakened to faith and reminded of the baptismal covenant, but in the most basic sense, at least, virtually all Europeans were Christians.

In the New World, by contrast, religious options abounded, vast spaces and the sense of newness shaped a reconceiving of time and place, and diligent missionaries could find baptized believers— and many more unbaptized people—miles from any house of worship and any opportunities for religious instruction. Like the members of other churches, Presbyterians arrived from Great Britain in large numbers and then scattered to settle far beyond the reach of organized churches.

The situation posed new problems for religious leaders who themselves were in short supply. Presbyterians had a tradition of learned clergy. Like other people shaped by the Reformed tradition, they believed that churches could not be formed without clergy, and that clergy needed extensive education—especially in scripture— before they were ready to be pastors. It took time, resources, and personnel, then, to establish the church in the colonies. Groups with less stringent expectations for clergy and members—those for whom religious experience and an inner sense of calling to ministry sufficed—adapted more readily to the American setting with its vast spaces and its urgency and pragmatism.

The geographic and social realities meant that basic questions of identity and mission loomed from the outset. What were the essentials to which one must hold in order to be Presbyterian? How could a tradition rooted in Calvin's understanding of divine providence meaningfully engage the other streams that coursed through American religious life? How could Presbyterianism be a viable option on the religious menu from which Americans chose their faith commitments? Could the tension between intellect and piety, between immediacy and patience in discipline and suffering, between works and grace be productive, or would it inevitably divide?

Further, was it the Presbyterian minister's primary duty to uphold truth? Or should he seek to augment membership by powers of persuasion? Could one balance Calvinist views of Providence and grace with a call to conversion? Benjamin Franklin's famous comment on the Philadelphia Presbyterian pastor who spent most of his time denouncing the errors of the non-Presbyterians around him pointed to a serious problem. What appropriately constituted the core of the message? How could enough clergy be recruited to keep pace with population growth, territorial expansion, and revival-generated opportunities? In his classic study of colonial Presbyterianism, Leonard Trinterud aptly summarized the situation:

> When all the old traditions, mores, conventions, and customs of the homeland which made for a formal adherence to religion and morality were sloughed off at the frontier, indifference to the Church and even to common morals, became everywhere evident. The church was weak. . . . Such prestige and influence as they were to have must be won by each minister individually.[5]

To some extent, then, location—especially the concept of space and the absence of imposing architectural reminders of time and tradition—made evangelism in the simplest sense of proclamation and persuasion essential to the future of the church. Traditional parish forms did not make sense in the New World. Hand in hand with revivalism, evangelism seemed a logical solution and a viable "technique" for the voluntary church. At the same time, however, the warnings of some Reformed believers that such culturally appropriate activity could easily undermine pivotal Presbyterian doctrines generated serious tensions.

None could dispute that Old World parish models did not apply in the New World, however, and American Presbyterians generally maintained only the loosest of official ties with their counterparts in the Old World. But a steady stream of immigrants nonetheless kept European influence alive, and it is not surprising that European controversies had repercussions in the American setting. Some immigrants attempted to ignore the factors pressing for change. These were like the people Sidney Mead labeled "reluctant pioneers" who looked nostalgically to the familiar Old World customs they had left behind.[6] Others were simply conservatives committed to time-honored ways. Such people demanded official subscription to specific doctrinal statements and attempted to transplant Old World customs into their new settings. They resisted adaptation because adaptation jeopardized their faith. Still others moved beyond the coastal cities where churches were readily available, however. They either left the church's purview or opted for the more casual revivalistic style of their neighbors. They fell under the sway of those who stressed the transforming power of the new birth and the tangible experience of the warmed heart.

Persistent tendencies toward presbyterian forms of organization among New England Puritans as well as growing numbers of Presbyterian immigrants steadily swelled the ranks of colonial Presbyterians. Their common commitment to the Westminster Standards at first held together the "New England element" and Scotch-Irish Presbyterians.

But in the 1720s, pressing questions of discipline, training, and communication could no longer be postponed. The tensions in the American colonies often followed ethnic lines, with the Scotch-Irish (concentrated around Philadelphia) demanding stricter discipline and subscription to the Westminster Standards, and New Yorkers and New Englanders opting for acceptance of the Bible alone as sufficient rule of faith and practice. In 1729, years of disagreement yielded an uneasy truce known as the Adopting Act, which distinguished between essential and nonessential articles of the Westminster Standards and allowed examining judicatories to assess a candidate's harmony with the intent of the Westminster Confession.[7]

THE FIRST GREAT AWAKENING

The truce did not last long, however; it was broken by the Great Awakening and the surfacing of a new group among the Scotch-Irish led by William Tennent. Tennent took his stand with those who insisted that Christian life must be grounded in personal conversion, nurtured by holiness of life, and disciplined by strict standards for admission to Communion. For Tennent and the party of Presbyterians who rallied to his view, the indispensable mark of Christianity was the experience of the new birth. Amid the furor of the Great Awakening that swept the colonies in the decades before the Revolution, the revival party grew dramatically. Some of the moments in the unfolding of the painful, divisive story that followed are well known, especially Gilbert Tennent's violation of ministerial courtesy by preaching uninvited within another's parish, and his incendiary sermon, "The Danger of an Unconverted Ministry."[8]

The New Side, typified by the Tennents, cast its lot with other supporters of the revival and organized the Synod of New York in 1745. Its leaders moved ahead with plans to found a college, for which they secured a charter as the College of New Jersey in 1746. The breach between Old Side and New Side was healed in 1758, at least superficially, on the terms of the supporters of revival. The revival party tended to emphasize evangelism and charity—the sharing of the gospel by word and deed.

Perhaps the best-known representative of this combination of revivalistic piety and evangelistic zeal was David Brainerd, who was one of several prodded by the fervor of the Great Awakening to engage in missionary work among Native Americans. Reformed believers had carried on missionary work among Indians for a century when Brainerd began his efforts. Evangelism among Native Americans did not spark the controversies that evangelism among white settlers did, especially when that evangelism went hand in hand with revivals. Ordained by the Presbytery of New York in 1742, Brainerd spent the next four years as a missionary to Indians in New York, Pennsylvania, and New Jersey. Near Trenton, New Jersey, he had his greatest success, baptizing thirty-eight Delaware Indians and establishing a church. He died prematurely in 1747 of tuberculosis at Jonathan Edwards's home in Northampton, Massachusetts. Edwards prepared Brainerd's *Diary* for publication, making the record of Brainerd's emotional, spiritual, and physical trials as a missionary both a heroic memoir and an inspirational classic. Through the *Diary,* Brainerd inspired generations of successors. It remains in print as an instructive indicator of a dimension of Presbyterian piety that is often overlooked.[9]

If Edwards's presentation of Brainerd's life came to epitomize a relationship between saintliness and evangelism with which many American Protestants resonated, the efforts of Samuel Davies offer a practical glimpse into how evangelism functioned in revivalistic Presbyterianism. Fresh from the revival fires that warmed the Middle Colonies, Davies headed south to the Virginia piedmont where in the

1740s and 1750s he put his considerable talents to good use. Preaching at various points across Hanover County, he called people to personal religious experience that, he insisted, stood at the core of Christian faith. His stunning success in evangelistic work led to a call to the presidency of the College of New Jersey (now Princeton University).[10]

Despite the impressive achievements of individual Presbyterians, however, throughout the colonial period, Presbyterian strength generally remained tied to ethnicity. Its presence in the South was weak, but at the end of the Revolution it stood poised to respond to the vast home missionary challenge that faced the churches of the emerging nation.

THE SECOND GREAT AWAKENING

That home missionary challenge came in the context of another wave of revivals that spanned several decades and that fanned the flames of foreign missionary fervor, too. This series of revivals known as the Second Great Awakening followed the Revolutionary War and manifested themselves differently in different contexts: sometimes they were boisterous, emotionally charged events; sometimes they were earnest, serious, and introspective; always they challenged the church to reevaluate its methods and test its vitality.[11]

The Cumberland Presbyterians
and the Campbellites

When it came to personal piety and heartfelt experience, some Presbyterians—especially in the West where camp meetings flourished—found their church sadly wanting. The early decades of the nineteenth century saw a kind of negative evangelism, with people who objected to the staid temper and rational bent of traditional Presbyterianism opting to secede and form other connections. The best-known secessions gave rise to vigorous new groups like the Cumberland Presbyterians.

Heirs to the Cane Ridge camp-meeting tradition begun by a

Presbyterian but exploited most ably by the Methodists, Cumberland Presbyterians were strong on evangelism and the new birth. They represented an attempt to adapt Presbyterianism to the frontier revivalism that seemed to move like an irresistible tide. They calculated pragmatically how to maintain and expand their witness to the gospel in ways that took into account the social, geographic, cultural, and religious realities that surrounded them. In the process, they alienated traditionalists who held to the need for extensive formal clerical education and creedal instruction for church members.

Throughout its American experience, the Reformed tradition has often held to clericalism in a way that has hampered its growth. Even if Presbyterian institutions had been able to meet the demand for clergy during the Second Great Awakening, it is not certain that those institutions could have provided graduates who could communicate effectively on the frontier. Competition was plentiful and tough: Baptist farmer preachers and Methodist circuit riders spoke the common idiom and were not distanced by birth or education from the people they exhorted. Further, Baptists and Methodists harvested and baptized converts without first instructing them in the formalities of doctrine as the Presbyterians did. For those in the Reformed tradition, evangelistic growth was slowed by expectations about the role of formally educated clergy. The pressures to adapt were considerable at times and played a role in some of the tradition's schisms.

The Campbellites (or Disciples of Christ) traced their roots directly to Scotch-Irish Presbyterianism. Campbellites presented a simple popular message that evangelized by appealing to the mind rather than galvanizing the emotions. Following their leaders, Thomas Campbell and especially his son, Alexander, they objected to the insistence of people like Samuel Miller that Presbyterianism as constituted around them replicated—or even resembled—the primitive church. While their theological understandings were shaped by Scottish Presbyterian debates, their restorationism resonated with the cultural openness toward re-formation, simplicity, and purity.

Such nineteenth-century offshoots of Presbyterianism splintered a recently formed national Presbyterian Church, created in

1789 by the forming of the first national General Assembly. By then, Presbyterians wielded significant cultural influence. Many held public office or engaged in professions that conferred cultural status.

Avenues of Cooperation

The opening of the frontier and the rapidity of westward migration posed an enormous challenge to all of the denominations. New denominations represented one way of dealing with denominational reactions to unprecedented challenges. Another response that made sense to some Presbyterians as well as to members of other denominations was cooperation for the extension of civilization and Christianity across vast territories. The people who pressed for the pooling of resources and personnel were responding to enormous pressures to preserve and extend American civilization. The belief that the West held the fate of the nation drove American Protestants to cooperate to civilize and Christianize (Protestantize) the vast new territories that opened for settlement after 1803. With other mainline Protestants, then, some Presbyterians viewed the West as both challenge and opportunity.

Revival fires fanned determination to evangelize the West. As noted, this commitment was much broader than Presbyterianism and more far-reaching than traditional Protestantism. It was augmented by the visions of reformers of every stripe, Christian and non-Christian, who saw in the West a chance to realize their dreams for perfecting society. A new surge of revivalism combined with utopian schemes and waves of Catholic immigration to pose troubling questions for Presbyterians, questions that focused tensions that had been close to the surface for years.

First came the Plan of Union, a scheme devised in 1801 to diffuse competition between Congregationalists and Presbyterians. On the surface, the plan made sense. These denominations had considerable doctrinal and historical continuity, and the enormity of the task in the American West dwarfed their differences. The plan permitted congregations of one denomination to call a pastor from the other, and it generally worked to Presbyterian advantage. From 1801 in New York and points west, more than five hundred

Congregationalist congregations became Presbyterian. Especially in New York, Ohio, Indiana, Illinois, Michigan, and Wisconsin, the two denominations essentially functioned as one.

Presbyterians in the former Middle Colonies provided a disproportionate share of the money and personnel that supported the joint efforts. They organized the Home Mission Society in 1812 to further the Plan of Union. As the continuing revival fed interest in foreign missions around the country and in many denominations, Presbyterians supported the predominantly Congregational American Board of Commissioners for Foreign Missions.

It is not surprising that some who cherished Presbyterian distinctives became noisy critics of the Plan of Union. By 1838, conservatives wanted to abandon it altogether. It represented yet another attempt to adapt to new realities, and it surfaced again the questions always inherent in denominational discussions about cooperation. Identity and distinctives seemed to some to be jeopardized by an American willingness to minimize differences in favor of acting out of common Christian faith. The Plan of Union was an early expression of the ecumenical bent that has marked parts of mainline Protestantism since. Historically, for some in any denomination, ecumenism raises more questions than it answers. Equally problematic to opponents of the Plan of Union (called Old School Presbyterians) was the apparent willingness on the part of proponents of the Plan (called New School Presbyterians) to tolerate diversity and sacrifice a degree of organizational cohesion in the interest of providing congregations where they did not exist. Though it surfaced over the years in many guises, the basic issue remained the same: it focused on what it meant to be Presbyterian. The task remained identifying the distinctives without which true Presbyterianism could not exist.

By the late 1830s, the Plan of Union was but one point of a growing multifaceted Old School–New School controversy. Equally troubling were a host of new societies—voluntary associations that sought interdenominational support for specific tasks. Large, ambitious projects launched by organizations such as the American Bible Society and the American Tract Society were supplemented by scores of less ambitious causes, some local and others national in scope—the Anti-Swearing League; temperance societies and the like—all intent on Christianizing the culture and making America "the salt of the earth." Add to the mix the emergence of a dynamic, determined lawyer-turned-evangelist, Charles G. Finney, and the stage was set for another schism.

Charles Finney and Revival Theology

Finney rose to fame in the 1820s and 1830s in the boom towns along the Erie Canal. After his tumultuous conversion experience in Adams, New York, Finney had studied for the ministry by reading theology with his pastor, a conservative Princeton graduate named George Gale. It soon became evident that Finney diverged from strict Westminster Standards at several points, but he was nonetheless licensed by the local St. Lawrence Presbytery. Finney found Gale's theology and the education and tradition it represented both offensive and immoral.

According to Finney, Christ had died for all rather than only the elect as traditional Calvinist theology insisted; people were damned for their own sins, not for Adam's as the Westminster Confession suggested; those who wanted to experience the new birth could do so by their own power rather than being totally dependent on God's initiative.

Finney was a popular preacher whose direct, blunt language called everyone to repentance. He devised measures to promote revivals, and he insisted that revivals were nothing more than the predictable results of the right use of the right means. He demanded that converts engage in the struggle for social change; his followers poured energy into the struggle against slavery and other forms of oppression. Not surprisingly, by the mid-1830s, Finney withdrew from his Presbyterian connections, but by then the denomination was headed toward schism.[12]

If the theology of popular evangelists like Finney was troublesome, yet another set of issues swirled around the approach to the task of evangelism. In the urgency to accomplish a task, individuals, societies, and denominations sometimes plunged ahead with little coordination or accountability. The claims—sometimes conflicting—of individual ministries, voluntary associations and denominational programs bombarded Presbyterians as they did all church members. The questions they raised surfaced some issues that had long agitated just beneath the surface.

While commending the zeal of individuals and acknowledging the responsibility of each to act in the best interests of others, Presbyterian leaders cautioned that the new, burgeoning evangelistic outreaches headed by individuals might well abuse power and resources. Voluntary associations tended to be cumbersome and to suggest that participation in the task was optional—"something we may take up or not, as it suits us, by uniting with some other organization," one writer put it.[13] Presbyterian conservatives made a strong case for evangelism as the task of the church whose members were "united not merely to observe the ordinances and hear the word, but also to teach and disciple others—to be the light of the world, the salt of the earth."[14] The problem was one of corporate responsibility versus individual enterprise. If the church was the "divinely appointed agency" for evangelizing the world, then the church needed to reclaim from voluntary associations the resources and the vision on which to act. Instead, the benevolent empire (as the interrelated configuration of voluntary associations was sometimes called) had assumed the church's responsibilities, and "activity and zeal" had been diverted from the church to parachurch organizations. People joined the church for "safe transportation to the heavenly shore" with little or no regard for the responsibility that stood at the heart of the church as community for common action in evangelism.[15]

The obvious solution, it seemed to some, was withdrawal from united action and commitment to denominational programs. The heated debate about missions agencies offers revealing insights into the tensions that challenged members of all the denominations, not just Presbyterians.

Presbyterians were seriously divided on the advisability of denominational over cooperative missionary efforts, both home and foreign. An 1831 report from the Board of Missions to the General Assembly advanced the view that every church should consider itself a missionary society, duty bound to present the gospel to everyone. The same report maintained, however, that there was room for both denominational missions and interdenominational missionary agencies. Presbyterians should publish, preach, and plant churches, bending every effort to extend Christianity at home and abroad, committing their resources first to denominational programs but supporting interdenominational efforts with discretionary money.[16] The endorsement was qualified, nonetheless: in no way could a voluntary association and a denominational missions board be considered equal. One had as its charge "a particular department of the kingdom of Christ"; the other the general spiritual welfare. One was regulated and consistent; the other more subject to changing circumstances and personnel.

Nineteenth-century Presbyterians knew that what was theoretically superior was not necessarily practicable: they would probably have chosen to supervise all American Protestant home missions, but that was clearly unrealistic. And so they followed—and supported with varying degrees of enthusiasm—the parallel efforts of the Home Missionary Society, a voluntary association, and of their own Board of Missions.

Missions among Native Americans
and African Americans

Work among various Native American tribes absorbed a considerable share of Presbyterian resources and offers an instructive case study. Although individual Presbyterians like David Brainerd and at least one synod—New York—actively supported Indian missions before 1800, the denomination's involvement began officially in 1800 when the General Assembly appointed a Standing Committee on Mission. Within a few years, Presbyterians supported outreaches among the Cherokees, Wyandottes, and the Six Nations. Gideon Blackburn became the denomination's first formally appointed missionary. He served among the Cherokees in Georgia for eight years until health problems forced his resignation.[17] Evangelism among the Indians remained under the supervision of the General Assembly until 1818 when the Presbyterian and Dutch Reformed Churches combined their vision and resources for outreach and formed the United Foreign Missionary Society. The joint venture lasted until 1826, when its nine missions and sixty missionaries came under the control of the Congregationalists' American Board of Commissioners for Foreign Missions. For the next five years, most Presbyterian evangelism among Native Americans was done under the auspices of the American Board.

In 1831, another option opened with the creation of the Western Missionary Society, formed by the Synod of Pittsburgh in response to pressure from Presbyterians who wanted denominationally controlled evangelistic outreaches. The Western Missionary Society was the forerunner of the Presbyterian Board of Foreign Missions that was organized by the 1837 General Assembly in Baltimore. The separation of the denomination into Old School and New School in 1838 limited the effectiveness of the Board until reunion in 1870. During the schism, New School resources went primarily to the American Board while the Old School worked through the Presbyterian Board.

Among the best-known New School Presbyterians to serve under the auspices of the American Board of Commissioners for Foreign Missions were Marcus and Narcissa Whitman. Early in 1835, Marcus Whitman, a medical doctor, and Samuel Parker, a minister, headed west to explore the Oregon Territory and prepare the way for a mission. By November, Marcus brought a favorable report east, and in March 1836, Marcus and his bride, Narcissa, and their colleagues Henry and Eliza Spalding left to establish missions under the American Board. The couples were newly married: the hazardous seven-month journey to Oregon Territory was their wedding trip. They arrived on September 2 at Fort Walla Walla where they separated. The Whitmans stayed nearby to work among the Cayuse at Waiilatpu; the Spaldings settled to the east among the Nez Percés at Lapwai.

The women's experience demonstrates the frustrations of women who sensed a call to ministry before the structures were in place to allow them to nurture their calls. A teacher, Narcissa applied for missionary appointment in 1834, but, as an unmarried woman, she was turned down. Her marriage to Marcus enabled her to go as his wife, however. Once in Oregon both Narcissa and Eliza Spalding became essential to the missions their husbands headed. They translated hymns and devotional literature, operated schools, worked among the women, and ministered to the suffering as well as to a steady stream of new white settlers. Among the first white women to cross the Rockies, they set an example for the countless pioneer women who followed. Personal difficulties took their toll—the accidental drowning of the Whitmans' two-year-old daughter; the loss of Narcissa's eyesight. But they faithfully plodded on until the fateful day in November 1847 when a band of Cayuse raided the Whitmans' mission and murdered the Whitmans and a dozen other whites on the property. The Spaldings barely escaped.[18]

The Board closed its Oregon missions, and twenty-four years passed before missionaries returned. Henry Spalding made the comeback. The lone survivor of the first missionary group, he headed back to Oregon in 1871, an old man eager to try once more. Indians who had loved him as a young missionary welcomed him warmly, and within a year he baptized 184 converts. When he died in 1874, 696 converts had been added to the roster and the mission was flourishing.[19]

The Whitman and Spalding stories raise another aspect of Protestant missionary efforts that has troubled many American denominations in the twentieth century. These missionaries failed to value the Native American cultures they encountered. Mission became as much a process of cultural conversion as of spiritual reorientation: missionaries expected converts to embrace Western ways as well as Christian faith. In devaluing native culture, missionaries sometimes also devalued non-Christian people. Mission activities brought into focus cultural conflicts that raised pressing questions for all Christians, especially from the nineteenth century when Western Protestants devoted themselves with particular zeal to circling the globe with the gospel.

Although their cultural assumptions troubled later generations, Narcissa Whitman and Eliza Spalding among others nonetheless served notice that Presbyterian women sought means to evangelize their world. Male missionaries recognized the importance of women's contributions to the prosecution of evangelistic outreaches too. Sheldon Jackson, a notably successful Presbyterian missionary in the Rocky Mountains and in Alaska, made it a point to get Presbyterian women's groups to support his efforts. From mid-century, he urged the formal organization of women's assistance, encouraging the creation of a women's home missions board. When the denomination did not move quickly enough to suit him, Jackson acted on his own, inviting interested women to a convention in New York. Such aggressive determination contributed in the end to the realization of his dream in the formation of the Women's Executive Committee of Home Missions of the Presbyterian Church.[20]

As Presbyterians worked to evangelize a growing nation, they—like other Christians—faced the particular challenges of spreading the gospel among African Americans. Their first efforts occurred in the small communities of free Blacks in northern cities, and, as in Methodism, followed the patterns of social separation that prevailed throughout the United States. The first Presbyterian church for Blacks was organized in Philadelphia by Archibald Alexander and an ex-slave, John Gloucester. Gloucester had been owned by Gideon Blackburn, the Presbyterian missionary to the Cherokee Indians whose views on slavery had evolved sufficiently over the years for him to free several of his slaves. The church, First African Presbyterian Church, was founded in 1807 with twenty-two members as a project of the Presbyterian Evangelical Society of Philadelphia. A similar congregation was established in New York in 1822, and others followed. Not surprisingly, Black pastors had difficulty meeting Presbyterian educational expectations and the additional problem of raising sufficient economic support.

CONCLUSION

Home and foreign evangelism played critical roles in the dramatic growth of Presbyterianism in the first half of the nineteenth century. Throughout American Presbyterian history, debates about evangelism helped focus deeply divisive issues that occasionally led to schism as Presbyterians faced the tension between intellect and emotion, Calvinism and revivalism. While they often failed to agree on method and assumptions, both sides in the disputes that channeled the tension always underscored the conviction that evangelism stood at the core of the mission of the church.

Debates about adapting to culture and to modernity have both energized and divided Christians throughout the American experience. In the past, people whose faith was formed by the Reformed tradition disagreed deeply about how adaptation might impact their sense of identity and mission. At particular historical moments, questions about the propriety of adaptation focused understandings of the importance and meaning of history, tradition, and heritage. In the current debate over adapting to the reality of a post-Christian America, its past offers the Reformed tradition both hope and caution. For those who see accommodation as the only solution to problems on every hand, the past amply demonstrates the dangers of unbridled adaptation to the culture. At the same time, the past reminds those who resist adaptation of the futility and potential divisiveness of resistance to change. Perhaps the best advice the past offers is to work constantly to cultivate a clear sense of identity and mission, for only clarity about these enables one to cherish one's own tradition and to cooperate effectively with others.

NOTES

1. Samuel Miller, *Manual of Presbytery* (Edinburgh: John Johnstone, 1842). Charles Hodge's published lecture "What Is Presbyterianism?" (Philadelphia: Presbyterian Board of Publication, 1855) makes no mention of evangelism, either. Rather, Presbyterianism is a system of doctrine and an organizational mechanism that Hodge, like Miller, maintained best approximated the New Testament model.

2. Charles G. Finney, *Memoirs of Rev. Charles G. Finney* (New York: Fleming H. Revell Co., 1876), 42–60.

3. Perhaps the best-known, though not necessarily the most typical, expression of this devotional piety is David Brainerd's diary, edited by Jonathan Edwards: *An Account of the Life of the Late Rev. Mr. David Brainerd* (Boston: D. Henchman, 1749). See David Brainerd, *The Life and Diary of David Brainerd,* ed. Jonathan Edwards: (Grand Rapids: Baker Book House, 1989).

4. For early Presbyterian history, see Leonard J. Trinterud, *The Forming of an American Tradition* (Philadelphia: Westminster Press, 1949).

5. Ibid., 36–37.

6. Sidney Mead, *The Lively Experiment: The Shaping of Christianity in America* (New York: Harper & Row, 1963).

7. Trinterud, *American Tradition,* 38–52.

8. Archibald Alexander, *Biographical Sketches of the Founder and Principal Alumni of the Log College* (Philadelphia: Presbyterian Board of Publication, 1851); Milton J Coalter, *Gilbert Tennent, Son of Thunder: A Case Study of Continental Pietism's Impact on the First Great Awakening in the Middle Colonies* (New York: Greenwood Press, 1986).

9. Brainerd, *An Account of the Life of the Late Rev. Mr. David Brainerd* (see note 3); Jonathan Edwards, *True Saints When Absent from the Body Are Present with the Lord* (Boston: D. Henchman, 1747).

10. Samuel Davies, *Sermons on Important Subjects* (Philadelphia: Robert Campbell, 1794); George William Pilcher, *Samuel Davies, Apostle of Dissent in Colonial Virginia* (Knoxville, Tenn.: University of Tennessee Press, 1971).

11. On the most famous of these, see Paul K. Conkin, *Cane Ridge: America's Pentecost* (Madison, Wis.: University of Wisconsin Press, 1990).

12. The most reliable edition of Finney's *Memoirs* is Richard Dupuis and Garth Rosell, eds., *The Memoirs of Charles G. Finney* (Grand Rapids: Zondervan Publishing House, 1989).

13. "Modes of Evangelization," *The Biblical Repertory and Princeton Review* 36 (July 1864): 398.

14. Ibid.

15. Ibid., 402.

16. "Domestic Missions: The Fifteenth Annual Report of the Board of Missions of the General Assembly of the Presbyterian Church, Presented May 1831; The Fifth Annual Report of the Home Missionary Society, Presented May 1831."

17. This information is culled from several sources: Belle M. Brain, *The Redemption of the Red Man: An Account of Presbyterian Missions to the North American Indians of the Present Day* (New York: Board of Home Missions of the Presbyterian Church in the U.S.A., 1904); Sherman Doyle, *Presbyterian Home Missions* (New York: Presbyterian Board of Home Missions, 1905); Michael C. Coleman, *Presbyterian Missionary Attitudes toward American Indians, 1837–1893* (Jackson, Miss.: University Press of Mississippi, 1985).

18. Narcissa Whitman became the subject of numerous Sunday school and library type inspirational books for youth. She and Marcus played political and cultural as well as religious roles in the opening of the Northwest, and the Western history literature on them is also extensive. A sampling of the literature includes Nard Jones, *The Great Command: The Story of Marcus and Narcissa Whitman and the Oregon Country Pioneers* (Boston: Little, Brown & Co., 1959); James Daugherty, *Marcus and Narcissa Whitman: Pioneers of Oregon* (New York: Viking Press, 1954); William A. Mowry, *Marcus Whitman and the Early Days of Oregon* (New York: Silver, Burdett & Co., 1901); Oliver Nixon, *How Marcus Whitman Saved Oregon: A True Romance*

of Patriotic Heroism, Christian Devotion and Final Martyrdom (Chicago: Star Publishing Co., 1895).

19. Brain, *Redemption of the Red Man*, 34.

20. J. Arthur Lazell, *Alaskan Apostle: The Life Story of Sheldon Jackson* (New York: Harper & Brothers, 1960), 208; Robert Laird Stewart, *Sheldon Jackson: Pathfinder and Prospector of the Missionary Vanguard in the Rocky Mountains and Alaska* (New York: Fleming H. Revell Co., 1908).

6. "Proclaim a Pure Gospel": Presbyterian Outreach from the Civil War to the Present

LOUIS B. WEEKS

On Sunday night, May 1, 1864, Archibald Alexander Hodge addressed the Board of Foreign Missions of the Presbyterian Church (Old School). He took as his text Genesis 49:10, the gathering of the people at Shiloh. Though the northern Presbyterians, as all other Americans, were deeply enmeshed in a civil war at the time, Hodge only mentioned it briefly. His major concern was the central duty of Christians to "evangelize the nations."

"Surely, then, woe is to us if we preach not the Gospel with all our might," he concluded. "Our duty is as simple and as single as that of the first evangelists. To proclaim a pure gospel by word and by life. The difference is only that we have a far grander theater, [and] are far nearer to the end."[1]

To those who consider American Presbyterianism as primarily a Protestant denomination divided between more conservative evangelicals and more liberal social activists, the sermon bears two striking features: it comes from a leader in the Old School denomination, the one noted for its scholastic Princeton theology rather than for its sympathy for revivals. It also plumbs simply but deeply the very center of Protestant evangelism.[2]

On neither account should the Hodge sermon seem unusual. By the 1860s most Old School as well as New School Presbyterians were unabashedly expressing their faith in the language of Zion, using the terms and contexts of the early church life as their own. Archibald Alexander Hodge assumed that there was one gospel and that it had identifiable substance. He saw the mission efforts of his day as consistent with the early mission efforts reported in the Acts of the Apostles and the letters of Paul. His sermon indicates belief in the imminent return of Jesus Christ, and as most Presbyterians of Hodge's time read the Bible, he assumed that the first Christians had all been evangelists. Therefore, modern Christians should follow in mission and evangelism.[3]

THE EVANGELICAL CORE OF
NINETEENTH-CENTURY PRESBYTERIAN FAITH

By the end of the Civil War, as cities grew, immigrants increased, and industrialization forced Americans into new patterns of work and family life, all the major streams of American Presbyterianism shared an evangelical faith. This was true despite the fact that southern Presbyterians had separated from the Presbyterian Church in the United States of America (PCUSA) during the Civil War, and the United Presbyterian Church of North America (UPCNA) did not merge with the PCUSA until well into the twentieth century.

The substance of Presbyterian faith was evangelical in the primary meanings of the expression. Presbyterians believed that Jesus Christ was "The Way, The Truth, and The Life" for humanity. They trusted in scripture as God's word about Jesus Christ and bearing God's authority. They believed the proclamation of the gospel was the primary duty of individual Christians and of the church in all that they did. They also supported various kinds of mission and revival efforts.[4]

This evangelical tenor to the nineteenth-century Presbyterian faith was not limited simply to the denominational leaders. As hundreds of congregational histories attest, mission groups arose spontaneously in individual churches. People heard about others in their own country and millions abroad who had not received or responded to the Christian gospel. Members of newly organized Sunday school classes of men and women, boys and girls contributed substantially to mission and evangelism funds. *The Christian Observer,* a widely read Presbyterian weekly magazine, noted in its "Religious Intelligence" column the number of persons added on profession of faith in large and small churches alike. Members and officers sought to proclaim a "pure gospel" by bringing others to Christ.[5]

Presbyterians supported some (but not all) revivals. In the words of the *Encyclopaedia of the Presbyterian Church in the United States of America* of 1884, "The Presbyterian Church has always been a friend of genuine revivals."[6] Although earlier in the century, debates had arisen and disciplinary actions had been taken in response to the efforts of Charles G. Finney, most presbyteries by 1875 welcomed revivalists such as Dwight L. Moody—if they could secure their services.[7]

This tabernacle evangelism of Moody and his song leader Ira Sankey had deep Presbyterian backing, though other mainstream denominations collaborated in sponsoring the events. In Philadelphia during 1875 and 1876, Presbyterian lay leaders were at the core of the effort. Thousands were converted, even more renewed in service, and new work among young men and young women grew as direct results of the campaign. Indirect results continued for months afterward, for revivals took place in congregations throughout the Presbytery of Philadelphia during 1876 and additions to presbytery rolls were greater than in any previous year. Moody also preached on the ethical implications of Christian faith, both personal and social. These grew from evangelical concern for people coming to believe the gospel through the witness of those who professed Christ.[8]

The support for revivals was matched by extensive domestic and foreign mission activities, mostly in the colonies of the European political powers. In 1875 the PCUSA sponsored 1,123 missionaries in domestic fields and more than two hundred others overseas. Reports spoke of extensive home mission programs in almost all the states and in six territories—Wyoming, Washington, Utah, New Mexico, Montana, and "Indian." Further, foreign missionaries served in countries and colonies now known as Mexico, Colombia, Brazil, Liberia, Iran, Chile, Lebanon, India, Pakistan, Thailand, Laos, China, Japan, and Italy. Missions among the immigrant Chinese and Jews attracted special attention, as did work among the Dakota, Creek, Seminole, Seneca, Chippewa, and Omaha tribal peoples.[9]

The PCUS General Assembly, still struggling in the midst of the devastation of the postwar South, challenged its presbyteries to secure evangelists and to pool money for their support. By 1875, twenty-four presbyteries had endorsed the "scheme" with some emphasizing city missionaries and others calling lay evangelists. The

PCUS engaged in evangelism among southern Blacks and in mutual mission with the Reformed Church in America. They had seventy missionaries in other lands—China, Brazil, Colombia, Italy, Greece, and Mexico.[10]

The UPCNA, less than a generation old itself in 1875, supported missionaries in China, India, Syria, and especially in Egypt, where their efforts had become concentrated. Their annual narrative of the state of religion lamented, "No special or remarkable revivals are reported," but added that thanks should be given for the "ordinary means of grace" in evangelistic endeavors. The General Assembly called on all congregations in the UPCNA to hold "special and protracted services of prayer and preaching" sometime during the upcoming church year.[11]

In 1875, new women's organizations for mission and evangelism were forming in the PCUSA, thereby expressing how both genders fervently wished to contribute to the enterprise. These women's boards and auxiliaries were emerging in different ways, the Foreign Mission Board report explained. It encouraged pastors and sessions to support the women in their efforts. Members of the other Presbyterian denominations followed soon after in recognizing the efforts of women for mission and endorsing them.[12]

To follow the pioneering ministry of Sheldon Jackson or the ministry in literature and hymnody of Elizabeth Prentiss is to view the depth and breadth of that evangelical center of Presbyterian belief. Jackson organized churches and fostered education at all levels throughout the American West, and he tolerated the ambiguity of serving as General Agent for Education in Alaska, a governmental responsibility, in order to further these causes together.[13] *Stepping Heavenward* (1869), *The Flower of the Family* (1853), and other books by Prentiss told stories of Christian witness and faith. Her hymn "More Love to Thee, O Christ" was part of *Golden Hours: Hymns and Songs of the Christian Life* (1871).[14]

Committed as they were to mission and evangelism, Presbyterians nevertheless assumed certain limits to their theology and involvement in witness. When ministers and evangelists moved beyond these limits, some found these boundaries too uncomfortable to remain in their denomination.

Albert B. Simpson personified both the evangelicalism among

Presbyterians and the testing of Presbyterian limits. Reared in a family of stern Canadian Presbyterians, Simpson became increasingly evangelical. In a long, written "covenant," Simpson dedicated himself to God in 1861. After seminary he ministered in Louisville, Kentucky. Simpson called on all the other Protestant pastors in the city to join him in supporting a revival by Major Whittle and "one of the sweetest of gospel singers, P. P. Bliss." After the 1874 revival, Simpson rented a public hall for his own evangelical lectures and services. The Thirteenth Street Presbyterian Church in New York City called him in 1879, and he began evangelistic work there. Two years later he resigned, and he left the Presbyterians to form what later became the Christian and Missionary Alliance. He and his followers espoused a "Four-Fold" theology that emphasized the personal experience of divine grace, the indwelling of the Holy Spirit in believers, supernatural healing for the faithful, and full sanctification in this life.[15]

Looking back, Simpson considered his Presbyterian parents to have been excessively strict, but he appreciated their teaching him scripture and the other religious knowledge he had gained. Although Simpson affirmed his Presbyterian roots, he finally felt constrained to leave the PCUSA.

Simpson perceived the Presbyterians as being willing to abide his beliefs but unwilling to commit themselves fully to the "radical and aggressive measures" God called him to undertake. He remained Presbyterian in his affirmation of the experience of divine grace and the indwelling of the Holy Spirit, but he moved beyond where most Presbyterians were willing to go when he affirmed the second half of his Four-Fold Gospel, namely, supernatural healing and full sanctification. In short, Presbyterian evangelicalism had distinct implicit, if not explicit, boundaries, and Simpson encountered them in both methods and theology.[16]

Simpson was the rare case among Presbyterians of the PCUSA, PCUS, or UPCNA. Most stayed within the limits of a deep, energetic evangelicalism. Comparatively well organized throughout the nineteenth century, PCUSA Presbyterians moved at the turn of the twentieth century to increase efficiency and influence for proclaiming the gospel. Those in the PCUS and UPCNA followed as quickly as money and Assembly policies would allow.

Programmatic Emphases in
Evangelism and Mission

In 1901, elder John H. Converse of Philadelphia, president of the Baldwin Locomotive Works, was made chair of a Special Committee on Evangelistic Work for the PCUSA. The committee engaged John Wilbur Chapman, already known in the city as an evangelist, to be its corresponding secretary and executive staff.[17] Chapman grew up in Indiana. He joined the Presbyterian Church at age sixteen. Ordained in 1882, he served Reformed and Presbyterian congregations in Albany, Philadelphia, and New York City, before being enlisted as the General Secretary of the new General Assembly Committee on Evangelism in 1902. Chapman assembled a team of Presbyterian revivalists that was largely supported by Converse, and he offered "The Simultaneous Plan" to cities in which large numbers of Presbyterian churches could participate.[18]

The energy and the reach of Chapman and his colleagues were considerable. To the 1903 General Assembly, the committee reported employment of fifty-one evangelists (ten of whom specialized in singing), visits to all the Presbyterian seminaries for worship, consultations, and instruction in evangelism, fifty-one conferences in various cities, days for special preaching and revival events in twoscore cities, and blanket permission for congregations, presbyteries, and pastors to engage in various methods of work appropriate to their own circumstances.[19]

In an exploration of the 1905 Portland and Seattle revivals led by Chapman, Dale Soden has called attention to the variety of modes employed by the evangelist and his colleagues. These included impromptu tent services, carefully designed worship experiences in the sanctuaries of major congregations, marches through targeted sections of the city, and small, specialized rallies and meetings for particular audiences. In Portland and Seattle, the impromptu tent services were frequently led by the Rev. Daniel Toy, a reformed alcoholic who described his past in sensational terms and preached with "a voice that tremble[d] with emotion."[20]

Most of the time, Chapman himself led worship in the churches, with Moody/Sankey style song services and carefully rehearsed choir music augmenting the sermons. Marches of adult Christians through red-light districts and of children through business districts, led by the Revs. C. T. Schaeffer and H. W. Stough, made news. The special meetings of working people led by the Rev. Charles Stelzle were part of an effort to pinpoint neglected segments of the cities' populations for evangelism. Stelzle also visited shops and working halls, met with delegates from labor unions, and enlisted ministerial representatives to continue cooperation with them.[21]

It is notable that Chapman teamed with Stelzle in designing and administering programs in evangelism. Charles Stelzle was the most visible Presbyterian in the social gospel movement. He was born and grew up in the Bowery section of New York City. Converted during a revival, he briefly attended Moody Bible Institute before receiving ordination. Stelzle specialized in relating to the developing labor unions in American urban areas. He also found time to focus PCUSA efforts on immigrants from Eastern Europe.[22]

If the PCUSA leaders saw evangelism and social witness as mutually compatible, they also saw Presbyterian evangelism as a complement to ecumenical collaboration. The 1904 Assembly authorized "such cooperation with other Evangelical denominations as may make it possible to move in a more marked way the cities of our land." In all efforts, moreover, good organization was seen as the basis of success.[23]

Some leaders in the PCUSA sought to revise the Westminster Confession of Faith. After unsuccessful attempts throughout the nineteenth century, and in response to overtures from many presbyteries, the PCUSA General Assembly of 1900 appointed a special committee, and they offered interpretive guides to mitigate the seeming harshness of doctrines concerning election, predestination, and atonement. In addition, they proposed new chapters: "Of the Holy Spirit," and "Of the Gospel of the Love of God and Missions." These adaptations of the creed were adopted overwhelmingly and were in place by 1904.[24]

The fact that Presbyterians altered their theological standards at the very time they adapted institutions to meet new circumstances indicates their awareness of an infrastructure for nurture and faith. Perhaps the organic metaphor of an "ecosystem" best describes the interaction of formal and informal conventions and institutions such as mission circles, informal Sunday schools, memorization of scripture and catechisms, family devotions, Sabbath observance, and a host of primary, secondary, and higher education locations upon which Presbyterians could focus attention. Gradually the formal institutions occupied more of that attention, as Presbyterians sought to meet the immense needs of people throughout the world and in their own country.[25]

The move to institutionalize evangelical Presbyterian Christianity seemed to pay off during the first decades of the twentieth century. Successive reports of first the PCUSA committee on evangelism and then those of the PCUS and the UPCNA showed "encouraging developments" on most fronts through the 1910s. In the words of the 1917 report for the PCUSA, "The evangelistic work of the Church . . . is becoming more efficient, because many Presbyteries have replaced the haphazard and isolated plans of individual churches with well-conceived Presbyterial plans."[26]

The move in global mission toward coordinated planning, careful management, hierarchies of control, and professionalization is more difficult to date. Several early signals suggest the change in emphasis. At the formation of the Laymen's Missionary Movement in 1896, Presbyterian elders and other so-called lay leaders met with counterparts from other mainline denominations and vowed to carry out "the evangelization of the world in this generation."[27] The 1898 General Assembly distinguished American "foreign missions" from the support of "native Churches" and encouraged the newer churches to become self-propagating, self-governing, and self-supporting.[28] It may have been that organization began to triumph over previously informal, familial, and paternally-oriented patterns of mission only when Robert E. Speer began his organizing work at the turn of the century.[29] Or it may not have occurred until 1910, when Presbyterian undergirding of the Edinburgh Mission Conference and the comity arrangements that stemmed from it meant programmatic considerations would have to predominate in Presbyterian missions because of the complexity of the responsibility.[30]

Whatever the exact date of this shift was, by the second decade of the twentieth century, programmatic mission efforts were fully implemented in the PCUSA. Comparison of the *Minutes* of the 1875 and the 1911 Assemblies shows startling differences in organization and emphasis regarding evangelism and mission. A "Narrative of the State of Religion" in 1875 began by talking about Presbyterian revivals, while the 1911 *Minutes* treat revivals as a part of the report of the Evangelism Department.[31] Again, the offices and incumbents for the PCUSA efforts in domestic mission are barely discernible in 1875, except for the secretary who signed the report and the treasurer who presented the budget. In 1911, those who served on the staff for Home Missions were named at the beginning of each section of the report—a Departmental Superintendent for each of Church and Labor, Immigrant, Church and Country Life, Indian Mission, Women's Board, and Young People's Work.[32]

The PCUS and the UPCNA lagged behind in time, but they took the same direction. Their mission and evangelism programs were eventually marked by specialization among personnel, attention to the supporting system, and management increasingly by those who made a career of it, rather than those who primarily served as pastors of congregations. The central "duty" Hodge had discerned from scripture for Presbyterians—"proclaiming a pure gospel by word and life"—had become one program of the church among several. Diminished if not forgotten was Hodge's millennial expectation of being "nearer to the end." Programmatic emphases meant that the church leaders planned and budgeted for the future more than they expected history's imminent culmination.[33]

Evangelism and mission were related to the recruiting of members for Presbyterian denominations, but they were certainly not exhausted in that enterprise. Evangelist E. O. Guerrant, who worked at the turn of the century in the poorest regions of Appalachia, told of converting men and women who could not bring themselves to form a Presbyterian congregation. He baptized some as Methodists, and he alerted a Baptist friend subsequently concerning the willingness of others to form a Baptist church. This attitude of considering people in need of salvation first and the expression of Christian loyalty in Presbyterian affiliation only secondarily also seems to have characterized a great portion of the mission work both domestic and foreign.[34]

It is important to note that Presbyterian leaders in evangelism and mission during the early decades of the twentieth century continued to be motivated primarily by an evangelical Christian worldview, even if it was shorn of its postmillennial expectations. Their public statements and sermons continued to sound very much like the words of Hodge. They understood the gospel as simply and purely an evangelical one—the proclamation of Jesus Christ in word and action. More important, most members, as well as most elders and ministers, seem generally to have maintained an evangelical Christian faith. However, the faith had been adapted, for now it focused on the amelioration of institutions and people in this world rather than on preparation for the coming of God's kingdom to displace this-worldly institutions. Charles Forman notes that missionaries began to rely less on their preaching and more on schools and hospitals during these decades.[35]

When San Francisco Seminary began its T. V. Moore Lectures, mission advocate and leader Robert E. Speer was the first speaker. He chose as his theme "When Christianity Was New," an exposition of the book of the Acts of the Apostles and other New Testament texts. As he introduced the topic, Speer said simply, "The conviction underlying these lectures is that the only true test of the legitimacy of any developments of the centuries which followed the first is their conformity to the authority of the New Testament."[36] As Bradley Longfield has recently shown, Speer epitomized liberal resistance to the fundamentalism of J. Gresham Machen. No one Presbyterian party held a corner on zeal for evangelism and mission.

By the same token, the theological changes under way in American Presbyterianism could not help but affect the priorities of mission and evangelism. Fundamentalist and modernist elements on the edges of centrist Presbyterian denominations became increasingly defined, increasingly vocal, and increasingly alienated. Presbyterian members and officers in the middle could not help but absorb some of the ambiguity and question some of the major tenets of the previously held evangelical theology.[37]

The methods of Billy Sunday, a charismatic but also theatrical preacher redolent of self-serving financial maneuvers, also caused new doubts in the minds of many Presbyterians about the efficacy of revivals. Licensed by the Presbytery of Chicago, Sunday used many of the techniques of Moody and Chapman. But when Sunday pronounced virulent anathemas on the German forces during World War I, and when some of his questionable finances came to light,

Presbyterians backed off from his evangelistic methods, considering them somehow tainted by their association with Sunday.[38]

Larger societal values and goals also doubtless impacted the changing Presbyterian consciousness. A Sheldon Jackson could organize new churches and expand mission efforts in new territories and be supported by almost all Presbyterians. Mission enterprises in other lands were surely linked to the expansionist mentality of Americans as well. As the American geographical frontier disappeared and expansionist tendencies subsided, certainly Presbyterians, like other Americans, were less clear about the need to "Christianize and civilize" the whole world. The frontiers of humanizing urban life for the poor, establishing partnerships with peoples in other nations for education and health, and working with other churches in evangelism and mission did have appeal, but they were more complex and less dramatic to many.[39]

CHANGES IN PROGRAMMATIC
MISSION AND EVANGELISM

As Milton J Coalter has pointed out, during the 1940s the PCUSA moved away from supporting evangelistic activities and municipal revival efforts at a denominational level and turned instead to encouraging person-to-person evangelism among the congregations. The New Life Movement of 1947–1950 was the first and the most successful program using the new emphases.[40] In response to changing American demography and the democratizing of higher educational opportunities, Presbyterians focused on new church development, training programs for laity and ministers, contacts from work and social events of members, visitation, and other tools to seek one million new Presbyterians by 1950, as well as other clear-cut goals. Their complex programs closely followed multiyear emphases in the UPCNA which had been in place since 1940. By 1950, PCUS programmatic innovations also gave its evangelistic efforts a higher profile in the life of the church, especially as instigated in a "Presbyterian Program of Progress," with a checklist of desired congregational activities.[41]

These programmatic changes seemed at first to bring benefits to the three denominations, just as efforts to increase organizational efficiency had done earlier in the century. More persons joined Presbyterian churches, especially on profession of faith, than had previously done so. As the decade of the 1950s wore on, however, denominational leaders in the PCUSA especially became skeptical of the efficacy of high-profile, programmatic evangelistic efforts. By the time of the union of the PCUSA and the UPCNA in 1958, denominational evangelism departmental staff no longer formulated program themselves but instead served regionally as participant-observers.

The PCUSA Board of National Missions united with the Board of American Missions of the UPCNA in the 1958 merger. In explaining the merger, Archibald Stewart and Hermann Morse, general secretaries respectively, stated the purposes of the new UPCUSA effort: "to provide a Christian ministry throughout our national domain," to serve human needs, to include "every variety of people," and to strengthen institutions of the new church. Though the statement still mentioned Presbyterian responsibility for "evangelization," that goal was not emphasized at all. The major thrusts of the statement emphasized maintaining and strengthening current members rather than winning new Christians or seeking to gain members.[42]

The 1958 National Missions Report still spoke of the "Front Lines of Mission Service" and the mission of evangelization, new church development and other avenues of outreach, but the companion report of the two foreign mission boards stressed mutual mission almost exclusively. The mission boards spoke at length about how leaders from emergent churches would be able to help American Presbyterians and others grow in faith. In addition, the report of the merging programs in Christian education showed little or no concern for evangelism and mission, save in the section on "Missionary Education," which spoke of teaching children in Presbyterian churches about foreign missions.[43]

A programmatic effort in the PCUS offered a "Presbyterian Mission to the Nation" beginning in 1960, with teams of Presbyterian leaders aiding pastors and members in scores of metropolitan areas to foster missions of "friendship," "Christian action," and "proclamation." Another initiative, "A Call to Repentance and Expectancy"

123

in 1965, sought to aid individual members of the PCUS energize their evangelistic efforts.[44]

Recent research by Thomas Berg indicates that this continuing Presbyterian focus on converting individuals during the 1940s and even the 1950s was shared by other members of the Federal Council of Churches and later the National Council of Churches (NCC). Elmer G. Homrighausen, dean of Princeton Theological Seminary, served as the chairman of a Board of Managers for an Evangelism Department in these organizations. Deeply influenced by the evangelistic work of Billy Graham, the National Council of Churches called Charles R. Templeton as evangelist. "Chuck" Templeton led rallies and revivals under NCC auspices for several years. According to Berg, however, cleavage between those seeking conversion of people and those increasingly concerned to foster direct political action caused the NCC to turn from its evangelistic enterprise in the early 1960s.[45]

As evangelism programs changed in tactics and organization, similar and far-reaching changes also characterized the mission programs of the Presbyterian denominations.[46] According to John Fitzmier and Randall Balmer, evangelical fervor characterized the PCUSA and PCUS leaders and the reports of the PCUSA Board of Foreign Missions during the 1930s. Both employed military metaphors to describe the work of the missionaries as well as the call to "occupy" all lands for Christ.[47]

Gradually, however, the language of mutuality in mission and of "fraternal workers" took center stage in missions vocabulary. Presbyterians adopted this activity and vocabulary in response to the expectations of indigenous Presbyterian and other Protestant church communions becoming autonomous or semiautonomous. These expectations were themselves harbingers of national and tribal independence movements throughout the developing world. Fitzmier and Balmer note also the increasingly self-critical reports of the mission boards and the ways American Presbyterians sought to subsidize the work of churches in emergent nations and to downplay their own role. The giving by Presbyterians and their congregations to support particular missionaries was also discouraged in favor of unified giving for the whole work of the church. The latter was easier to distribute and considered more responsible in such partnership arrangements. Some of the funds continued to support Presbyterian missionaries, but increasing percentages went to enable indigenous churches to develop their own leadership. Moreover, the language of mission "partnership" supplanted the rhetoric of personal, self-sacrificial service.[48]

Programmatically, in 1958 the new UPCUSA replaced the boards of foreign missions, which had overseen efforts in the two previous denominations, with a Commission on Ecumenical Mission and Relations (COEMAR). Theodore Gill points to the 1962 Montreat consultation on missions in the PCUS as moving that denomination in the same direction.[49]

Did the programmatic changes perceived as necessary reflect a diminution in the evangelical interests and zeal for missions on the part of Presbyterians, or did they help foster the loss? Whatever the relationship, by the mid-1960s at denominational levels and also in many, if not most, congregations Presbyterians did not see the same pure gospel Hodge had seen—a simple, evangelical core to the Christian faith.

THE PARTIAL ECLIPSE OF
PRESBYTERIAN EVANGELICALISM

The PCUS Board of Church Extension noted in 1964 "the apparent lack of evangelistic concern which has fallen like a miasmic fog."[50] Many of the formal and informal institutions, which previously had supported missions and evangelism and together had formed the ecosystem transmitting faith to future generations, were in decline or had almost altogether disappeared—Sabbath observance, Sunday schools, close relationships with Presbyterian colleges, and mutually reinforcing congregational and campus ministry ties, for example.

Certainly by the 1970s the evangelical heritage of Presbyterians did not weigh heavily on the hearts and minds of most members and officers in the churches.[51] A *Presbyterian Panel* poll in 1976 indicated that the great majority of Presbyterian members, pastors, and elders wanted their congregations involved in a denominational effort to reach "people without the Gospel" who resided in the United States. But only about one in three members said that she or he was willing to spend a moderate amount of time in such an enterprise.

Moreover, only one fourth of the members, a third of the elders, and half the pastors would definitely encourage their congregations to provide additional financial support should that effort be directed to reaching people without the gospel in another land.[52]

Other findings showed similar sentiments regarding evangelism and mission. Few members and elders said the church helped them much in sharing their faith with others. Few said they did it regularly. Only a quarter of the members, a third of the elders, and sixty percent of the pastors stated that they were willing to receive training and further education in evangelism and mission. Only about a third of the members and elders said they were willing to visit newcomers in their own communities.[53]

The responses of Presbyterians to a questionnaire might not prove diminished interest in mission and evangelism, but one imagines far different responses from such a sampling in 1875, 1910, or even 1955.

Increasingly, Presbyterians in the 1970s and 1980s used the term "mission" to describe all their activities, even the maintenance functions in denominational life. When the UPCUSA and the PCUS reunited and formed the Presbyterian Church (U.S.A.) in 1983, a Structural Design for Mission was adopted. Basic principles enunciated in the design included the commitment "to share the love of Christ with the world." But other principles were now put alongside it—"the unity of the church," "tradition and flexibility," "partnership," etc. To the Global Mission Unit was assigned Christian outreach, and to the Evangelism and Church Development Unit was given responsibility for "implementing strategies for evangelism and Christian witness." The descriptions of most other units and related bodies used the term "mission," but only in its most general sense, and they said nothing about evangelism or outreach, except in helping people economically or supporting their civil rights.[54]

Certainly many causes contributed to the shift among Presbyterians away from centering on evangelism and toward calling everything mission, away from attention to salvation for those not Christian and toward ecumenical relations with partner churches. Scholars have pointed, for example, to the diminution of Americans' ebullience and tendencies toward imperialism.[55] Others have seen the then prevalent neo-orthodox theology as a major ingredient in the change, since it offered a chastened view of human (even churchly) motivation as well as a more modest assessment of the part people play in bringing about the will of God.[56] Still others have pointed to the loosening of religious authority and the processes of secularization and modernization as major factors in bringing about the change. Recently, Nathan Hatch has argued that Presbyterians and other so-called mainstream Protestants backed away from their earlier populism and embraced the values of an American cultural elite, leaving to the fundamentalists and others identification with the American masses.[57]

Although many Presbyterians supported the work of Billy Graham and other evangelists of the 1940s and 1950s, many criticized their easy alliances with political leaders and their relatively superficial assessments of the Soviet Union, the People's Republic of China, and other communist countries as satanic in nature. Graham seemed to many much more like a Billy Sunday than a Wilbur Chapman or a Moody. But perhaps they also confused him with less scrupulous revivalists that they also saw on television, the new medium for mass communication. For whatever reasons, many Presbyterians became anti-revival and reluctant to speak openly of the evangelization of others during this time period.[58]

In the lives of many if not most Presbyterians, there was not a "pure gospel," a primary commitment to mission and evangelism. Instead, attention to evangelism and mission had become elements, sometime peripheral elements, in their faith. The "pure gospel" of Hodge seemed to become a complex gospel. Gone was the optimism of Hodge that Christ would soon claim his own or redeem the world, or that all would be confronted with the gospel and perhaps affirm the Christian faith.[59]

A number of particular congregations in the PCUSA maintained a central emphasis on evangelism and mission, though emphases began to change for them as well during the 1960s. Others have come increasingly to emphasize outreach and sought faithfully to witness in their communities by word and deed. A few presbyteries never lost their energy for forming new congregations to serve growing neighborhoods. But one can discern the eclipse of an evangelical commitment in the actions of most governing bodies and many congregations.[60]

127

On the other hand, General Assemblies of the PC(USA) have consistently named evangelism as a primary Christian purpose, usually balancing it with peacemaking. Evangelism area staff for the PC(USA) and for several synods have developed resources to assist congregations and presbyteries. Consultants on new church development have offered plans for different kinds of new church developments, for example; and they have trained teams of ministers and lay leaders to lead presbyteries in "Institutes for Congregational Evangelism." They have also assembled a list of "gifted speakers and renewal leaders" who constitute a "College of Evangelists," available for special services throughout the PC(USA).[61] In a statement adopted by the 1991 General Assembly, "Turn to the Living God: Evangelism in Jesus Christ's Way," Presbyterians committed themselves formally to "witness to God's grace and love in Jesus Christ." "Together," it declared, "we will invite people of every tribe, tongue, people, and nation to join us in turning to the living God."[62]

CONCLUSION

During the Civil War, evangelically minded Presbyterian denominations heard clear statements of the evangelical core of the Christian gospel as the basis for mission activity. In very recent decades, although evangelism and mission have remained a part of the expressed faith for Presbyterians and of the PC(USA), they are seen as central to fewer members, and probably a minority. No "pure gospel," such as that articulated by Hodge, is motivating present Presbyterian activity in mission.

What happened among Presbyterians and more widely in American life to influence or contribute to this change between the Civil War and the present? Among the Presbyterians, theology, programmatic structures, and location in American society certainly underwent drastic changes. Moreover, the denominational infrastructure diminished in vitality, with those elements that remained under severe strain.

More widely, American society settled its geographic frontiers. It came to terms with its blatant strains of imperialism, and its predominant cultures became at least more self-critical and less energetic. The public perception of evangelism changed. Some functions of mission within the United States were taken over by government social service agencies, foreign aid programs, and international relief organizations. Individualism may have increased. Secular values came to predominate in higher education. On and on goes the list of interactive changes, and together they influenced the language and values of Presbyterians imperceptibly but thoroughly.

Presbyterians certainly have adapted through the decades. They have changed emphases and vocabulary in both evangelism and global mission in response to the myriad changes in the world within which the church has sought to minister.

But the institutionalization of both evangelism and mission within the Presbyterian denominations also had a profound effect. Milton Coalter, speaking of the PCUSA in the early 1900s, points to the irony that "evangelism had previously been assumed to be the motive force and purpose behind all programs of the church's many boards and agencies. Now it became one of several ecclesiastical offices of technical expertise."[63] The same process characterized mission efforts, both domestic and global. The professionalization and the institutionalization took their toll, especially as efficiency and mutuality in mission decreased Presbyterian members' personal knowledge of the recipients of their benevolence funds and the causes to which their donations were applied.

On the other hand, perhaps insightful Presbyterians have all along maintained, and even voiced, an evangelical gospel and a devotion to mission, despite the changes and the temptations to focus on less crucial issues. Perhaps that is how the PC(USA) has managed to keep naming evangelism as one of its priorities. Perhaps that is why the heritage keeps drawing Presbyterians, challenging them to interpret the faith appropriately for succeeding generations.

NOTES

1. Archibald Alexander Hodge, "The Gathering of the People to Shiloh" (New York: Mission House, 1864), bound with Presbyterian Church in the United States of America Foreign Mission Reports, 1863–1870, in the Ernest White Library, Louisville Presbyterian Theological Seminary. Also

included in the collection are similar sermons from other eminent Presbyterian divines of the day.

2. The classic statement concerning development of a split between conservative evangelicals and social activists in American Protestantism is by Jean Miller Schmidt, published two decades after her dissertation as *Souls, or the Social Order: The Two-Party System in American Protestantism* (Brooklyn, N.Y.: Carlson Publishing, 1991). She dates the split between 1890 and 1915 and traces the divisions from that time. This research indicates much later, and somewhat different, divisions; but her pioneering work remains extremely important.

3. According to George Marsden, "almost all nineteenth-century American Protestants had been evangelical." By that Marsden meant they were almost all part of the "coalition reflecting a merger of pietist and Reformed heritages" that issued from the Enlightenment. See George Marsden, "Fundamentalism and American Evangelicalism," in *The Variety of American Evangelicalism,* ed. Donald W. Dayton and Robert K. Johnson (Knoxville, Tenn.: University of Tennessee Press, 1991), 23. This book is extremely helpful in sorting out the various streams of American evangelicalism and the opening chapter by Timothy Weber offers a particularly useful taxonomy. Hodge and most Presbyterians of the time were "classical evangelicals" in that they followed the doctrines of the Reformation and were loyal to the "ultimate authority of the Bible, justification by faith, an Augustinian anthropology, and usually a substitutionary view of the atonement." Timothy Weber, "Premillennialism and the Branches of Evangelicalism," in *Variety of American Evangelicalism,* 12.

4. Randall Balmer gives a somewhat different definition in *Mine Eyes Have Seen the Glory: A Journey into the Evangelical Subculture in America* (New York: Oxford University Press, 1989), x. He says that they still subscribed to the rudiments of Luther's theology, albeit with more freedom in worship than the reformer envisioned, a "spiritual rebirth," generally an emphasis on the inerrancy of scripture, and a proselyting zeal. On the relationship between evangelicalism and activism, see Glenn Hewitt, *Regeneration and Morality: A Study of Charles Finney, Charles Hodge, John W. Nevin, and Horace Bushnell* (Brooklyn, N.Y.: Carlson Publishing, 1991). His portrait of Charles Hodge also points to the difference between him and his son, Archibald Alexander Hodge. Charles Hodge thought little of revivals, according to Hewitt.

5. The *Christian Observer* also included lengthy items under "Religious News" and "Contributions." See "A Remarkable Work of Grace," *Christian Observer,* June 3, 1891, 5, for a description of evangelist Sam Jones in Chattanooga, Tennessee; and also "Evangelistic Work in Ouachita Presbytery," *Christian Observer,* July 15, 1891, 4.

6. "Revivals," in *Encyclopaedia of the Presbyterian Church in the United States of America* (Philadelphia: Presbyterian Encyclopaedia Publishing

Co., 1884), 756. The whole book is a treasure trove of glimpses into the piety of the time. Archibald Alexander Hodge, for example, is not noted particularly for his evangelistic faith. Others, like Alexander Jelly, are noted for being "evangelical, earnest, and eloquent" in his preaching (379). Julia A Graham of New York City, a leader in establishing the Ladies Board of Mission, was said to have "died working for missions" (273). Frederick Starr, minister in St. Louis, received "the divine blessing" in his ministry of fostering outreach (855).

7. See William R. Moody, *D. L. Moody* (New York: Garland Publishing, 1931, 1988).

8. Lefferts Loetscher, "Presbyterians and Revivals in Philadelphia since 1875," *Pennsylvania Magazine of History and Biography,* January 1944, 54–92. For another, equally engaging episode, see Darrel M. Robertson, *The Chicago Revival, 1876.*

9. Presbyterian Church in the United States of America, *Fifth Annual Report on Home Missions* (1875), 1, 6, 74; and Presbyterian Church in the United States of America, *Thirty-Eighth Annual Report of the Board of Foreign Missions,* 3–86.

10. Presbyterian Church in the United States, General Assembly, *Minutes,* 1875, 219, 247, 254. (Hereafter cited as PCUS, GA, *Minutes.*) In the "Narrative on the State of Religion," the Moderator reported that membership was increasing and "evangelistic labors" were improving, 247.

11. United Presbyterian Church of North America, General Assembly, *Minutes,* 1875, 170–81. (Hereafter cited as UPCNA, GA, *Minutes.*)

12. Ibid., 105. See also Presbyterian Church in the United States of America, General Assembly, *Minutes,* 1875, Part I, 106–9, for reports of various societies. (Hereafter cited as PCUSA, GA, *Minutes.*)

13. Elizabeth A. Tower, *Reading, Religion, and Reindeer: Sheldon Jackson's Legacy to Alaska* (Anchorage, Alaska: Roundtree, 1988), 33–55. See also Arthur Lazell, *Alaska Apostle: The Life Story of Sheldon Jackson* (New York: Harper& Brothers, 1960).

14. Ola Elizabeth Winslow, "Elizabeth Payson Prentiss," in *Notable American Women,* ed. Edward T. James (Cambridge, Mass.: Harvard University Press, 1971), vol. 3, 95, 96. Prentiss's hymn itself captures significantly the spirit of the evangelical Presbyterians of the period.

15. A. E. Thompson, *A. B. Simpson: His Life and Work* (Harrisburg, Pa.: Christian Publications, 1960), esp. 50–62.

16. Ibid., 75–98.

17. PCUSA, GA, *Minutes,* 1901, Part I, 119, 170, 171. As that committee reported in 1902, it is interesting to note the variety in methods and strategies they embraced: "Decision Days in Sabbath Schools," special meetings, evangelistic services, presbyterial visitation, "personal work," "open air and tent preaching," and others. PCUSA, GA, *Minutes,* 1902, Part I, 33–37.

18. PCUSA, GA, *Minutes,* 1902, Part I, 33, 34.

19. PCUSA, GA, *Minutes,* 1903, Part I, 42, 43, 74.

20. Dale E. Soden, "Anatomy of a Presbyterian Urban Revival: J. W. Chapman in the Pacific Northwest," *American Presbyterians* 64 (Spring 1986): 49–57.

21. Ibid., 54.

22. On Charles Stelzle, see his autobiography, *Son of the Bowery* (New York: George H. Doran Co., 1926). Stelzle is frequently credited as the major Presbyterian leader in the social gospel movement. Dislocated in the bureaucratic reorganization of 1920, he became embittered regarding the ability of the PCUSA to meet the challenges of America's industrialization and a further chapter in his autobiography is called "Why I Left the Church" (though he remained at least on paper a member of New York City Presbytery until his death).

23. PCUSA, GA, *Minutes,* 1904, Part I, 36.

24. Lefferts A. Loetscher, *The Broadening Church: A Study of the Theological Issues in the Presbyterian Church since 1869* (Philadelphia: University of Pennsylvania Press, 1954), 80ff.

25. On Presbyterian ecosystems, see Milton J Coalter, John M. Mulder, and Louis B. Weeks, *The Re-Forming Tradition: Presbyterians and Mainstream Protestantism* (Louisville, Ky.: Westminster/John Knox Press, 1992), 88, 89, 193, 194, 220–22, 261–72.

26. PCUSA, GA, *Minutes,* 1917, Part I, 427.

27. Ruth Rouse and Stephen C. Neill, *A History of the Ecumenical Movement,* 2d ed. (Philadelphia: Westminster Press, 1967), 353.

28. PCUSA, GA, *Minutes,* 1898, Part I, 73.

29. Robert E. Speer, *Christ and Life* (New York: Fleming H. Revell Co., 1901); see also his *Christianity and the Nations* (New York: Fleming H. Revell Co., 1910).

30. William R. Hutchison, "Americans in World Mission: Revision and Realignment," in *Altered Landscapes: Christianity in America, 1935–1985,* ed. David W. Lotz, Donald W. Shriver, Jr., and John F. Wilson (Grand Rapids: Wm. B. Eerdmans Publishing Co., 1989), 155–70. Hutchison sees the watershed in the movement from "foreign missions" to "world mission," both theologically and organizationally, from Edinburgh.

31. PCUSA, GA, *Minutes,* 1911, Part I, 17.

32. Ibid., 1–18.

33. T. Watson Street, *On the Growing Edge of the Church* (Richmond: John Knox Press, 1965), 118–20. A colleague, Joel Alvis, has copies of "Stock Certificates" issued by the Executive Committee for Foreign Missions of the PCUS to the Men's Bible Class, St. Paul's Presbyterian Church, St. Pauls, North Carolina. This illustrates how Presbyterians in the 1915–16 church year envisioned their support of Japanese missions as owning "shares" in that work.

34. Edward O. Guerrant, *The Soul Winner* (Lexington, Ky.: A. B. Morton, 1896), 250, 251.

35. In my research for *Kentucky Presbyterians* (Atlanta: John Knox Press, 1983), I was struck time and again by the evangelical energy of elders and of women who led the church during the first two decades of the twentieth century. I called the period "Into Heartland Presbyterianism." See also Charles W. Forman, "Evangelism in Global Mission: The American Presbyterian Experience" (paper presented at the Faithful Witness Conference, Louisville Presbyterian Theological Seminary, Louisville, Ky., March 18–19, 1993).

36. Robert E. Speer, *When Christianity Was New* (New York: Fleming H. Revell Co., 1939), 6. Interestingly, chapters dealt particularly with issues of economics and race as well as with Christology and other religions. Speer still saw evangelism and mission in their integration rather than their competitiveness. See also PCUSA, GA, *Minutes,* 1932, Part II, 153–55, for more evidence of this continuing focus. The Board of National Missions gathered groups of seventy who dedicated themselves "to carry forward (presumably) from the early church's efforts) the difficult but glorious task of bringing individuals into saving relationship with Jesus Christ."

37. Loetscher, *The Broadening Church;* Bradley J. Longfield, *The Presbyterian Controversy: Fundamentalists, Modernists, and Moderates* (New York: Oxford University Press, 1991).

38. Lyle W. Dorsett, *Billy Sunday and the Redemption of Urban America* (Grand Rapids: Wm. B. Eerdmans Publishing Co., 1991). In Roger A. Bruns, *Preacher: Billy Sunday and Big-Time American Evangelism* (New York: W. W. Norton & Co., 1992), 305, Bruns quotes this characterization of Sunday's ministry by a Washington, D.C., editorialist: "Billy Sunday is the man who put 'riot' in patriot."

39. Robert T. Handy described the end of the dream of a "Christian America" in "The Second Disestablishment," *A Christian America* (New York: Oxford University Press, 1984), 159–84.

40. Milton J Coalter, "Presbyterian Evangelism: A Case of Parallel Allegiances Diverging," in *The Diversity of Discipleship: Presbyterians and Twentieth-Century Christian Witness,* ed. Milton J Coalter, John M. Mulder, and Louis B. Weeks (Louisville, Ky.: Westminster/John Knox Press, 1991), 33–54.

41. Ibid., 42–46.

42. United Presbyterian Church in the U.S.A., General Assembly, *Minutes,* 1958, Part II, 110–21. (Hereafter cited as UPCUSA, GA, *Minutes.*)

43. UPCUSA, GA, *Minutes,* 1958, Part II, 1. See also the report from the PCUSA and UPCNA foreign mission boards, UPCUSA, GA, *Minutes,* 1958, Part II, 32, 61.

44. PCUS, GA, *Minutes,* 1965, pp. 48–51.

45. Thomas Berg, "'Proclaiming Together'? From Convergence to Divergence in Mainline and Evangelical Evangelism, 1945–67," *Religion and American Culture,* forthcoming.

46. One difference is interesting in the location of the reports of the PCUSA (UPCUSA following 1958) and the PCUS. The Board of National Ministries ("Home Mission" and related activities) always reported first for the PCUSA, while the Board of Foreign Mission (after the PCUS established one) reported first for the southern church. This first place in the annual reports of the church may also have indicated something about priorities.

47. John R. Fitzmier and Randall Balmer, "A Poultice for the Bite of the Cobra: The Hocking Report and Presbyterian Missions in the Middle Decades of the Twentieth Century," in *Diversity of Discipleship,* 105–25.

48. Ibid., 114–18.

49. Theodore A. Gill, Jr., "American Presbyterians in the Global Ecumenical Movement," in *Diversity of Discipleship,* 126–48.

50. PCUS, GA, *Minutes,* 1964, Part II, 44.

51. Street, *On the Growing Edge of the Church,* 15. See also Peter Berger, "American Religion: Conservative Upsurge, Liberal Prospects," in *Liberal Protestantism: Realities and Prospects,* ed. Robert Michaelson and Wade Clark Roof (New York: Pilgrim Press, 1986), 35.

52. UPCUSA, Research Division of the Support Agency, *Presbyterian Panel,* May 1976, 1–34. "One-to-One Evangelism," the current program emphasized at the time in the UPCUSA, received affirmation from only 7 percent of the members and elders and only 6 percent affirmation from pastors when respondents were asked to name good ways of reaching those without the gospel. Ibid., 24.

53. Ibid.

54. Presbyterian Church (U.S.A.), "Structural Design for Mission," (1991). (Hereafter cited as PC(USA).)

55. Robert Moats Miller, *American Protestantism and Social Issues (1919–1934)* (Chapel Hill, N.C.: University of North Carolina Press, 1958).

56. James H. Moorhead, "Redefining Confessionalism: American Presbyterians in the Twentieth Century," in *The Confessional Mosaic: Presbyterians and Twentieth-Century Theology,* ed. Milton J Coalter, John M. Mulder, and Louis B. Weeks (Louisville: Westminster/John Knox Press, 1990), 59–83.

57. Nathan O. Hatch, *The Democratization of American Christianity* (New Haven, Conn.: Yale University Press, 1991). See also William Hutchison, ed., *Between the Times: The Travail of the Protestant Establishment in America, 1900–1960* (New York: Cambridge University Press, 1989).

58. Marshall Frady, *Billy Graham: A Parable of American Righteousness* (Boston: Little, Brown & Co., 1979), 236–39.

59. Note the multiplex themes of the Brief Statement of Reformed Faith (1990). PC(USA), GA, *Minutes,* 1990, Part I, 267–69. The new denomination in 1983 had adopted a *Book of Confessions* following the pattern of the larger UPCUSA partner in the union; the matter of confessional authority itself had become more complex. Indeed, many in the PC(USA)

employ the first three theological chapters in the *Book of Order* rather than the *Book of Confessions* when deciding questions of confessional authority!

60. R. Stephen Warner, *New Wine in Old Wineskins: Evangelicals and Liberals in a Small-Town Church* (Berkeley, Calif.: University of California Press, 1987). See also Grace Ann Goodman, *Rocking the Ark: Nine Case Studies of Traditional Churches in the Process of Change* (New York: Division of Evangelism, UPCUSA, 1968).

61. Robert H. Bullock, Jr., "Twentieth-Century Presbyterian New Church Development: A Critical Period, 1940–1980," in *Diversity of Discipleship*, 55–82.

62. "Institute for Congregational Evangelism," "Commitment to Evangelism," and "Introducing Presbyterian Global Evangelism" (1992), promotional literature from the Evangelism and Congregational Development Ministry Unit.

63. Coalter, "Presbyterian Evangelism," 39.

7. Social Witness and Evangelism: Complementary or Competing Priorities?

RONALD C. WHITE, JR.

American Presbyterians adopted two mission priorities for the 1990s: evangelism and justice.[1] But announcing these priorities is not the same as clarifying their relationship. Although evangelism has been the priority for most of the history of American Presbyterians, social witness has achieved increasing prominence in the twentieth century, with a dramatic expansion developing in the 1960s. For many Presbyterians, evangelism and justice are complementary mandates of the gospel of Christ. But all too often misunderstandings about evangelism and justice have helped fuel divisions within modern Presbyterianism.

THE PRESBYTERIAN HERITAGE

At the beginning of the twentieth century, Presbyterians unanimously agreed that evangelism was the primary task of their church. This consensus was a heritage bequeathed by nineteenth-century Presbyterians. Evangelism had no programmatic center in the church because it was assumed to be at the heart of every program. Until the beginning of this century there were no committees or departments of evangelism. Ministries to Blacks, Native Americans, and varieties of immigrants in cities were supported, but the first priority in these ministries was always evangelism.

Evangelism was not a program; it was a perspective. Just as each Christian was expected to be a witness to the grace of God experienced in Christ, so too the mandate for each part of the church was to proclaim that Jesus Christ was Lord of all of life.

The central discussion about social witness in the nineteenth century was the debate over slavery. Presbyterians were deeply divided over whether the church, as an institution, should make a strong social witness about slavery. In 1818 the General Assembly issued one of the strongest antislavery statements by any national church body: "We consider the voluntary enslaving of one part of the human race by another . . . utterly inconsistent with the law of God . . . and . . . totally irreconcilable with the spirit and principles of the Gospel of Christ."[2] This vigorous statement, however, was not enforced on the constituent parts of the church.

Antislavery efforts were more vibrant among the revival-minded New School party than the Old School. By the 1830s the discussion of slavery had become so acrimonious that the General Assembly in 1836 voted: "Resolved that this whole subject be indefinitely postponed." The debate over slavery was one of the issues in the Old School–New School division of 1837. From the 1830s onward Presbyterians often pursued their antislavery interests through the structures of voluntary societies such as the American Antislavery Society and the American and Foreign Antislavery Society.[3] But in 1864 conflict over the issue of slavery among others led Southern Presbyterians to separate from the Presbyterian Church in the United states of America (PCUSA) by forming the Presbyterian Church in the United States (PCUS).

NEW BEGINNINGS IN THE NEW CENTURY

Evangelism and justice ministries both made fresh beginnings in the new century. In 1901 the PCUSA General Assembly appointed a Special Committee on Evangelistic Work to spearhead a new effort in evangelism. In 1903 the Board of Home Missions created a Workingmen's Department. What became known as the Department of Church and Labor was the first social action agency established in an American denomination. In appointing John Wilbur Chapman as corresponding secretary for evangelism, the denomination secured one of its leading pastors and the best-known evangelist in the church.[4] The initial thrust of the committee was to deploy evangelists around the country. By 1903 the committee reported 682 requests for the services of fifty-one evangelists. The evangelists responded by traveling 121,324 miles and holding 10,597 services in 470 cities.[5] This energetic campaign was not, however, evangelism by committee. Chapman was the leader and sparkplug.

In these same years a new beginning was launched in social witness. The initiative grew out of the vision of a remarkable Presbyterian, Charles Lemuel Thompson.[6] Under his leadership the Board of Home Missions "recognized the new occasions which teach new duties and began to organize departments for lines of work which had not up to that time challenged serious attention."[7] Thompson had spent his ministry in growing cities, and he determined that the Board of Home Missions needed to respond to the needs of urban people.

In 1903 Thompson appointed Charles Stelzle to minister among workingmen. Stelzle was uniquely suited for his new assignment. A "son of the Bowery," Stelzle grew up on New York's Lower East Side. Quitting school at age ten, he became a journeyman machinist. Proud of his membership in the American Federation of Labor, he was a lifelong friend of labor. Stelzle lacked a formal education, except for a year spent at the Moody Bible Institute. Here he learned how to be a street evangelist, training that he said prepared him for speaking at factories and street meetings.

From his position as head of the Department of Church and Labor, Stelzle carried on a dual campaign to sensitize the Presbyterian Church to the labor movement and to convince workingmen that a socially sensitive Christianity was friendly to them.[8] Within a few years the success of the Department of Church and Labor sparked the founding of other departments. The Department of Immigration grew out of Stelzle's department, and the Department of the Church and Country Life brought sociological expertise to the changes in rural life and ministry.

In 1910 Stelzle reported on the methods of social witness that had been "tested and proven effective" in the first seven years of the department. These included popular mass meetings for workingmen on Sunday afternoons, a weekly article in nearly three hundred labor newspapers, "shop meeting campaigns," the observance of Labor Sunday (which received the official endorsement of the American Federation of Labor), conferences between employers and employees, and a correspondence course in "Applied Christianity." Stelzle's methods reveal an evangelistic impulse as well as efforts to understand the problems and grievances of laborers.[9]

Thompson was pleased with Stelzle's passion for the city and for laboring people, calling the Department of Church and Labor "a precedent among American Protestant Churches and . . . the most statesmanlike thing to be chronicled in the history of American Protestantism in the past decade."[10] Although the northern Presbyterian Church was generally less receptive to the social gospel than other mainstream Protestant denominations, Stelzle represented a vigorous expression of the social gospel's concern for the new problems of the cities and laboring people.

The PCUSA made its first pronouncement on economic issues at the 1910 General Assembly. The report spoke to fourteen areas, including "the obligations of wealth," "a more equitable distribution of wealth," and recommendations for safeguarding the labor force, including the protection of children and women. The report was vigorous if moderate in tone, but it set a precedent that would be referred to again and again in future Assemblies.[11]

Taken together, Chapman, Stelzle, and Thompson represented a shared vision about evangelism and social witness in these pioneering years. They saw their roles as complementary. Dale Soden observes how Chapman and Stelzle teamed together at various evangelistic meetings. In revivals in Portland and Seattle in 1905 Stelzle visited factories, convened meetings with labor leaders, and led meetings for working people.[12]

Chapman's evangelistic aim was to reach all of society, but the goal was never fully realized. The Philadelphia *Public Ledger* reported in 1908 that "the audiences were made up of the respectable middle class." Chapman was not satisfied with the outreach to the marginalized of society. To remedy this "incompleteness," Chapman teamed with Stelzle and others like William Asher and his wife "who visited and worked among groups in saloons and prisons." The Ashers' ministry meant that many of these persons "attended the central meetings and signified their conversion."[13]

Chapman resigned in 1911, Stelzle in 1913, and Thompson in 1914. The esteem in which Chapman and Thompson were held resulted in each being elected Moderator of the General Assembly.

Stelzle, on the other hand, was acclaimed, but his resignation came under pressure. Critics charged that his ministry was not sufficiently evangelistic.

Thompson acknowledged that as each new department was added it "awakened a good deal of criticism among men of limited vision, who had not yet learned what the Church should do under the new conditions to christianize our nation." City work "was criticized because it took social and housing conditions into account in taking the gospel to crowded populations." The immigration work, which noted "bad conditions," was criticized for "interfering with secular and political matters which must not be tolerated." Thompson's opinion was that "we were feeling our way toward this new yet old interpretation of the gospel."[14]

THE SPIRITUALITY OF THE CHURCH

In 1902, the PCUS established the Permanent Committee on Evangelistic Work. J. Ernest Thacker, pastor of the Second Presbyterian Church of Norfolk, was hired in 1909 as the first General Secretary of the Committee on Evangelistic Work. Thacker was an evangelist who led campaigns for judicatories, but unlike Chapman, he never was asked to direct a nationally financed denominational program.[15]

In the PCUS, evangelism was more decentralized, but its centrality was clear. Ernest Trice Thompson declared, "The Southern Presbyterian Church became more evangelistic minded than ever before, and evangelism, the `winning of souls,' came to be widely accepted as the primary, and sometimes it seemed, as enthusiasts of the day claimed it to be, the sole mission of the church."[16]

Whenever the PCUS attempted to talk about social issues one perspective determined the substance of the conversation. The doctrine known as the "Spirituality of the Church" had been defined by James Henley Thornwell in the years leading up to the Civil War. Thornwell taught that the church should not speak where the scripture did not speak. "The silence of Scripture is as real a prohibition as a positive injunction to abstain. Where God has not commanded, the Church has no jurisdiction."[17] In the first General Assembly of the PCUS, Thornwell declared, "The provinces of the church and state are perfectly distinct, and the one has no right to usurp the jurisdiction of the other. . . . They are planets moving in different orbits, and unless each is confined to its own track, the consequences may be . . . disastrous."[18]

The doctrine of the Spirituality of the Church set the parameters for discussion of social issues in the PCUS for the next seventy years. Occasionally the church struggled with this doctrine, most notably in its support for the temperance movement, but by and large, the southern Presbyterian church courts were silent regarding social issues.

The most vibrant social witness in the PCUS grew out of the efforts of courageous individuals. Alexander J. McKelway, as editor of the *Presbyterian Standard* (1898–1905), wrote about the injuries that were becoming commonplace in the industrialization that was changing the South. McKelway became best known nationally as an opponent of child labor. He used his columns to support a North Carolina child labor law. After resigning as editor in 1906, he became Secretary of the National Child Labor Committee. Because of his efforts and the backing of the American Federation of Labor, every Southern state had an age-and-hour law by 1912.[19] McKelway helped spur a resolution on child labor adopted by the General Assembly in 1908. This was the only resolution relating to labor and business passed by the General Assembly in this period.[20]

What was constant, in both northern and southern Presbyterianism, was the primacy of evangelism. Each agency announced its evangelistic intent in report after report. In 1906, the PCUSA's Board of Home Missions stated, "Our Church is historically an evangelistic church." In 1922, on the occasion of 120 years of the same Board of Home Missions, "primacy" was given to four elements in home missions. But it noted, "The first and most important is evangelism." After restructuring in 1923 this sentiment was reiterated in 1924: "The Boards now merged in National Missions were all created to do the work of evangelism."[21]

Similarly in the PCUS, Home Missions stated in 1918 that "the first service rendered a community . . . is necessarily in the sphere of evangelism." This priority remained clear in 1932: "Evangelism is at the center of Home Missions as well as of the whole Church."[22]

THE INCORPORATION OF
THE CHURCH'S WITNESS

In 1923 the PCUSA reorganized the General Assembly. This structural change was part of a growing movement of incorporation in American life. Alan Trachtenberg defines incorporation as "the emergence of a changed, more tightly structured society with new hierarchies of control."[23] Louis B. Weeks has argued that Presbyterians "have been especially susceptible" to the process of incorporation throughout the twentieth century. Incorporation brought the benefits of efficiency. Formal departments replaced voluntary committees. Positions that were volunteer became full-time and paid. Experts were increasingly sought.[24]

Incorporation in 1923 meant that ten boards, which had been semiautonomous, were consolidated into four boards. Representatives of the Committee on Evangelism expressed fear that they would lose their visibility in the new structure. They were told that there was no intention of diminishing either their importance or their visibility.[25] The intention in the fourfold division was to create a new decentralized structure.

Taking cognizance of reorganization and the danger of a Division of Evangelism, the Board of Home Missions reemphasized the priority of evangelism in its 1924 annual report. "From one point of view a separate Division of Evangelism seems an anachronism. The Board has *only* Divisions of Evangelism, whatever their respective fields of service may be."[26] The message was clear. Every division's priority was to be evangelism.

Despite the best of intentions, however, restructuring did bring about an important change in the way evangelism would henceforth be viewed. As Milton J Coalter has pointed out, on the one hand, the rhetoric about evangelism continued to insist that it was the central priority for every part of the church. Yet, in restructuring, the church created a Division of Evangelism. The story of modern Presbyterians often involves unintended results. This unintended result was that evangelism, lip service to the contrary, was now simply one division among many.[27]

The irony of the next decade was that at the very time that

evangelism found a fixed place in the national structure, it "decentralized its operations and assumed a more passive administrative style." The church under Chapman's leadership had previously enjoyed strong national direction in evangelism, but now initiative shifted to the presbyteries and synods. The theory was to move away from high-profile evangelists and trust the church's own pastors with evangelism in their locales. There was much to commend in this intention. But in the 1920s and 1930s the church either grew slowly or lost members. It is hard to assess responsibility for this slide or slump because other denominations experienced similar problems.[28]

One result of this unexpected flatness in church growth was a questioning of the previously unquestioned purpose and method of evangelism. Beginning in the 1930s discussions of social witness would refer often to both the inadequacy of evangelistic strategies and the shallow faith exemplified in church life during the 1920s.

The development of incorporation in the PCUS took a different shape in these same years. Thornwell's understanding of the Spirituality of the Church assumed that the church had no warrant for creating boards since such structures went beyond scripture. Thus PCUS governing bodies initiated mission directly, and efforts in evangelism were done by executive committees of the General Assembly. As southerners, members of the PCUS feared centralization even more than did their northern brothers and sisters. Consequently even these executive committees were dispersed geographically.[29]

RETHINKING THE SHAPE OF SOCIAL WITNESS

A central thrust of the variegated social gospel movement focused attention on both social sin and social salvation. This emphasis grew out of experience with the problems of urbanization and industrialization. Social gospel leaders, learning from the developing social sciences, recognized that social analysis needed to move beyond an atomistic understanding, wherein society was nothing more than a collection of individuals, and move instead toward an organic understanding of society, one that acknowledged the whole as interrelated and more than the sum of the parts.

Reinhold Niebuhr, a critic of aspects of the social gospel, presented a more sophisticated analysis in his 1932 publication *Moral Man and Immoral Society*. Niebuhr attempted to understand how moral individuals could participate in immoral social structures. If the problem was corporate, then the response needed to be corporate as well. The church needed to bring its corporate voice and power to bear in society. Churches needed to learn how to exercise power. Niebuhr encouraged the churches to "use the forces of nature to defeat nature."[30]

By the early 1930s Protestant churches were beginning to ask in new ways the old question, Where and how must the church speak and act? The option was often posed in this way, Do Presbyterians act individually in society or does the church act collectively? These questions were asked during the debate over slavery, but the pressures of twentieth-century society and the formulations of Niebuhr and others raised the questions with a new urgency.

The Synod of Virginia evidenced a readiness to rethink the shape of social witness in 1932 when the mandate of the Committee on Interracial Relations was broadened by a new name, the Committee on Moral and Social Welfare. In its first report the committee addressed interracial relations, temperance, war and peace, crime, and the church and economic order. The committee stated that "the Christian message is a message not only of personal regeneration, but of social redemption."[31] The synod report was distributed widely throughout the church. This single report "did more to stir the church to action than anything else which had been done."[32]

At the 1933 PCUS Assembly, debate over the disappointing results of the current three-year plan on evangelism included a discussion of the need for an increased social witness. Stuart R. Oglesby offered a resolution that asked why God had not brought revival to the church. He acknowledged that "increasing moral laxity among the people and the lack of social responsibility is widespread throughout our church."[33] In the midst of the discussion of the evangelism strategy's shortcomings, the General Assembly voted 134 to 39 to establish the Committee on Moral and Social Welfare. The next morning ruling elder Samuel M. Wilson called the proposal un-Presbyterian, "a new and unwarranted departure from our historic practices." Wilson went so far as to ask the Assembly to strike out both the debate and the vote from the records. The Assembly took the unusual action of doing so by a vote of 137 to 99.[34]

But discussion of the church's role in social witness could not be stifled. In 1929 Walter Lingle had delivered the James Sprunt Lectures at Union Theological Seminary in Virginia on "The Bible and Social Problems." He enlisted John Calvin to argue that we cannot admit two spheres of action: "Born anew through grace, the Calvinist has a mission to carry out: namely, to purify the life of the community and to uplift the state."[35]

What about the courts of the church? Reviewing Thornwell's words from 1861, Lingle offered the opinion that "it is a great deal easier to write this doctrine down on paper than it is to carry it into practice in actual life."[36] Despite Thornwell's positing two distinct spheres, Lingle observed that in fact church members are also members of the state.

Lingle also pointed to the statement in the PCUS's *Book of Order* that "the sole functions of the Church, as a kingdom and government distinct from the civil commonwealth, are to *proclaim,* to *administer,* and to *enforce* the law of Christ revealed in the Scriptures." Rather than accepting the interpretation that forbade the church from speaking on social issues, Lingle suggested that the law of Christ "contains some clear teachings" on social issues. As for the conflict between capital and labor, Lingle admitted that "some people seem to think that the Church has nothing to do with this conflict." He countered, "The Bible has much to say about money, about the withholding of wages, and about the oppression of the poor." Further, "It is the right and the duty of the Church to proclaim these great principles to her members and to insist that they practice these teachings in all their business and industrial relationships."[37]

In 1933 four synods—Georgia, Louisiana, North Carolina, and West Virginia—established committees on moral and social welfare. In 1934 the General Assembly considered such a committee again. This time the idea prevailed by a vote of 163 to 103. After nearly three quarters of a century, during which time the doctrine of the Spirituality of the Church had blocked any such action, the PCUS started down a road in which there was no turning back.[38]

The General Assembly's Permanent Committee on Moral and Social Welfare presented its first report in 1935. The report represented a reinterpretation of the church's position on the Spirituality of the Church. It stated that "the Church in fulfillment of its spiritual function must interpret and present Christ's ideal for the individual and for society."[39] The report made clear that "the first duty" of the followers of Jesus "is to win men to Christ." However, it asserted that evangelism is "only the beginning of the Church's task. It is the foundation on which all other work of the Church must be built, but it cannot stop with the foundation."[40]

In 1945 the Assembly gave the committee permission to speak to the church directly in its own name. The next year a full-time director was appointed for the first time. At the same time the committee's name was changed to the Council on Christian Relations.

In just fourteen years a remarkable change had occurred in southern Presbyterian social witness. Sparked by a few courageous individuals, the church reinterpreted its social witness. From a witness exclusively through individuals, it finally sanctioned a witness by church bodies. From the study of issues by a committee often unsure of its future, a permanent structure and a full-time salaried director was put in place to support the efforts of social witness at the end of World War II.

In a time frame paralleling the new departures in the southern church, a rethinking of the shape of social witness occurred in the PCUSA. The Board of National Missions appointed a permanent committee on Social and Industrial Relations in 1931.[41] Speaking about "The Ground of our Social Obligation," the committee's 1931 report stated that "the really urgent social questions of today are those related to the family, race prejudice, lawlessness, capital and labor, peace and war. These combine to voice a strong demand for a social interpretation and practice of the Gospel."[42]

The following year the committee presented a strongly worded indictment of "The Present Economic Situation." Commenting on the suffering across the country, the report called for a different measurement henceforth of the integrity of the economic order: "Nothing is more obvious than that the present economic order is now on probation and its continued existence and justification must be found not in the wealth produced or the power gained, but in its contribution to social service and social justice."[43]

Even as the voices of social action were being heard in the

1930s, words affirming that evangelism and social witness belonged together were also voiced. In 1935 the Assembly declared, "There is one Gospel of Christ. It cannot be reduced to an equation of evangelism plus social gospel, considering the two as separate; each fails if it stands alone." The next year a recommendation asked the Committee on Social Education and Action to work with Evangelism to "keep before people the Gospel of the new heart and the new Christian life in social service."[44]

EVANGELISM: SEEDTIME AND HARVEST

The Protestant churches in America entered a harvesttime of growth following World War II. Elmer G. Homrighausen, dean of Princeton Theological Seminary, spoke of a "revival of evangelistic fervor" at a meeting of the National Council of Churches. John A. Mackay, who had come to his position of president at Princeton Seminary after missionary service in Latin America, called for a renewal of "evangelistic fervor" in order to encounter the "spiritual vacuum" of the postwar years.[45]

In the PCUSA during the 1940s a National Commission on Evangelism was established, and it promised to give evangelism a higher profile. George Sweazey became the new General Secretary of the Unit on Evangelism in 1945. The Board of National Missions produced a report in 1946, "Threshold of Peace," that stated, "Basic to all other concerns is Christian evangelism." At the 1948 General Assembly in Seattle the Assembly set a goal of one million new members by 1950.[46] The major vehicle would be the New Life Movement. Its goal was for the church to enter the next half century "revived" and ready to face the future. The results were impressive. As shown in Table 1, almost 650,000 members were received or restored in the three-year campaign.[47]

The New Life Movement evoked tremendous enthusiasm. The movement seemed to be reaching into every area of the church's life. Included in this outreach was the conviction: "It expresses itself in the work of Social Education and Action."[48] Of the voices in evangelism that sought to combine soul winning and social action, many embraced the notion that the best approach was dependence

TABLE 1
Members Received or Restored (PCUSA)

Reception by	Average Pre–New Life Year	*1947	New Life Movement Years 1948	1949
Profession and Reaffirmation	86,957	111,765	117,476	118,985
Certificate	55,247	83,125	84,838	87,114
Restoration	12,726	16,560	13,975	14,745
Total	154,930	211,450	216,289	220,844

Estimated

on converted individuals rather than a social strategy of direct action. This was the strategy of Billy Graham, who in the 1950s gained support from mainline denominations. George Sweazey encouraged this kind of social witness, cautioning that the "only way Christian principles can be put into the social order is to put them into the hearts of one member of society after another."[49]

Evangelism in the PCUS also enjoyed more prominence at the Assembly level in the mid-1940s although nothing on the scale of the New Life Movement was attempted. A Presbyterian Program of Progress focused on what congregations could do each year. The result was a membership growth in the years 1947–1952 that was greater than the previous twenty years combined.[50]

In the midst of these successes a shift was taking place in the understanding of evangelism. Earlier in the century the appeal was for persons to become Christians and then join the church. By 1950 more and more emphasis was placed on church membership.

Although the New Life Movement was seen as a harbinger of things to come, in some ways it was a trumpet sounding at the end of an era. The evangelism report of 1952 summed it up by saying, "Evangelism has too much been thought of as a peculiar activity by peculiar people at irregular times. The New Life program has been bringing the conception of evangelism as a normal activity for all church people all the time."[51] The intention was to move away from the high-profile revivalism of the past. The strategy was to give evangelism back to the ordinary person. What was not admitted was the incredible energy of national staff that fueled the New Life Movement even if the focus was on congregational evangelism.

The style henceforth would be person-to-person evangelism. The staff would function more as resource persons than evangelists. They would be consultants for different kinds of churches rather than constructing a model for the whole church. Following the crest of the New Life Movement, many welcomed this less aggressive posture adopted at the end of the 1950s.

As the PCUS approached its centennial in 1961, the evangelism division prepared a campaign that would capture the dynamism of the New Life Movement. A "Presbyterian Mission to the Nation" was a high-profile campaign, ranging from preaching cavalcades in eighty metropolitan centers to programs at the congregational level.[52]

One part of the campaign attempted to link evangelism and action. A *Manual on a Mission of Christian Action* stated that "every particular church witnesses to Christ through its members, both individually and corporately, both in word and deed." It argued that "a congregation bears a united witness that has not been generally acknowledged because its importance is so little understood." The manual declared that "God's people bear a collective witness, and that they witness through deed as well as word." The goal was to focus more on deeds than words. "What is *done* may actually speak louder and be heard more widely than what is said, however important the spoken word must be."[53]

The Presbyterian Mission to the Nation was well planned, but the results were disappointing. The PCUS did not experience growth. Instead, it declined in both professions of faith and net growth. Public southern jeremiads quickly followed in the early 1960s.

THE ASCENDANCY OF SOCIAL WITNESS

In the supposedly placid 1950s there were challenges to the notion that saved individuals were all that was needed to save society. The most persistent attack came from Reinhold Niebuhr. He attacked the Billy Graham notion of evangelism as underestimating the power of sin, and he criticized the easy crusade commitments that did not last. Although Niebuhr was especially hard on Graham, his critique included more theologically sophisticated notions of social witness relying on individual conversion.[54]

An answer to Niebuhr came swiftly from Homrighausen, one of the foremost interpreters of neo-orthodoxy. In an article in the *Christian Century,* Homrighausen indicted neo-orthodox theology as "hesitant and weak in calling persons to a positive faith." Homrighausen believed that Graham "says in sincerity" what thousands are longing to hear. Homrighausen threw down the gauntlet to "the neo-orthodox with all their accumulation of intelligence about the Bible and history and personality." If this be fundamentalism, Homrighausen challenged, "Where are the new orthodox evangelists?"[55]

In the late 1950s the momentum from the New Life Movement waned just as theological voices and the civil rights movement forced the church to reexamine its social strategy. It was in these years that the evangelism and social justice agendas of the church passed by each other without speaking.

One can see in the annual reports that evangelism, once the highest priority of the church, was slipping from Assembly view. At the same time social witness became more prominent with each passing Assembly. Racial justice dominated reports starting in the late 1950s. In the 1958 Assembly, which united the PCUSA and the United Presbyterian Church of North America to form the United Presbyterian Church in the United States of America (UPCUSA), a special report was issued: "Racial Integration in the Churches."[56]

In 1961 the Social Education and Action Committee became the Department of Church and Society. The department was charged with providing information on social issues to the Assembly. In succeeding Assemblies, reports were prepared about a host of important issues. The first report was thirty-five pages. The volume of the reports grew rapidly: 42 pages in 1965, 76 pages in 1967, 116 pages in 1970, and 216 pages in 1972. There were continuing reports on race, the war in Vietnam, and special reports on human sexuality and the environment. The long report in 1972 dealt with open housing and residential desegregation, civil strife in Pakistan, proposed selective service regulations, the Economic Opportunity Act, school busing, the value-added tax, Vietnam, justice and prisoners, and population policy.[57]

Social witness was undergirded by a panoply of theological voices. In 1965 Harvey Cox's *The Secular City* celebrated secularization and urged the church to respond to the world's needs on the world's terms. In the late 1960s Black theology challenged the churches to take seriously Black history, culture, and experience as norms for theological reflection and action. In the 1970s feminist theology challenged traditional male understandings in both theology and ethics. Liberation theologies from Latin America, Asia, and Africa focused attention on praxis—the practice or action of the church—rather than belief as the test of faithfulness.

Responding to social justice impulses from both outside and inside the church, the scope of Presbyterian social justice structures expanded. Social witness grew beyond the Department of Church and Society in the UPCUSA. In 1968 the UPCUSA's Commission on Religion and Race became the Council on Church and Race. Increasingly, the Church and Society Committee called for a strategy focusing on a ministry to social structures. The problem went beyond the individual. Thus in the 1968 Church and Society report was heard: "There is a meanness and malice built into the institutions and structures of our society."[58]

In the late 1970s a new commitment to peacemaking was growing out of the agony of Vietnam. The UPCUSA was a national leader among American churches. The initiative Peacemaking: The Believers' Calling in 1980 asked sessions to sign a commitment to peacemaking.[59]

A REDEFINITION OF EVANGELISM

In the midst of 1960s activism, evangelism became a target. Evangelism was criticized as being too rooted in revivalistic forms of the past. The methods of evangelism were said to be manipulative. But the real brunt of the criticism was against "words." The critics said that less proclamation and more demonstration were called for. Words were opposed to deeds, and the question was heard in many circles, Could you witness to Christ without mentioning his name?

As social issues came to dominate the UPCUSA Assembly, the Division of Evangelism responded. In 1964 the division produced its first policy statement dealing with a social issue: "Evangelism and Race." The report declared, "The Church cannot proclaim the

Christian gospel of reconciliation and ignore, evade, or play down the question of race."[60]

The redefinition of evangelism went forward rapidly with the appointment in 1966 of George T. Peters as secretary. Peters's prior interests differed from his predecessors. The bulk of his experience had not been in evangelism but in justice ministries. He had chaired the Assembly's Social Education and Action Committee from 1952 to 1955 and the Church and Society Committee of the Synod of California from 1960 to 1964.[61]

Of his new assignment Peters said, "Almost everything the Church has been about must be rethought and recast, from its vocabulary to its mission." As for the strategy of ministry, "the Church will have to learn how to listen and how to serve."[62]

At the 1967 General Assembly in Portland the Division of Evangelism presented a policy statement that dramatically redefined the meaning and scope of evangelism. Titled "Mission and Evangelism," the statement declared, "All evangelism is mission but all mission is not necessarily evangelism. Christians often are engaged in the mission of the Church without any explicit or self-conscious verbal reference to their being Christian or to the teachings of Christ. They simply allow their Christ-formed consciences and concerns to cooperate with, and to take part with, other men, whether Christians, Jews, humanists, or atheists, in working for the welfare of other men."[63]

This statement shifted the emphasis from words to deeds. The impulse of the social gospel had been to move the church to deeds of love and justice. For years the reports of the Social Education and Action committees had stressed the need for action. But neither the social gospel nor the Social Education and Action committees would have advocated deeds without words.

In these years evangelism literature and reports begin to speak of Christ's counsel that those who would lose their lives for his sake would save them. In the face of membership loss it was suggested that the winnowing of membership might actually prove a cure. The call was for a model of self-sacrifice. When questions were asked about why people were leaving, a typical answer was contained in a report to the 1968 General Assembly: "The Church has no warrant for substituting a statistical graph for a cross." As true as this statement might be, Coalter is on target when he declares, "The logic of self-sacrifice proved impenetrable to questioning from these statistical losses."[64]

The intensity of the debate about evangelism and church membership was reflected in the Evangelism report for 1969. The Assembly was told that "members of the Council on Evangelism and the staff of the Division approached their work with some trepidation and a deepened sense of the seriousness and complexity of their task." In their report they warned about "the inherent dangers" in various "modes of evangelism." On the one hand, concern for unbelievers should not "isolate the individual from meaningful relationship to the whole world for which Christ died." On the other hand, "the struggle to transform the structures of the community, church and nation" can lead to a "preoccupation with the political ramifications of structural change to the neglect of an affirmation of the Lordship of Christ over individuals." On the whole, the report was a balanced attempt to speak to what it called "a growing 'polarization' within the church."[65]

UPCUSA membership began a precipitous decline in 1966, with an average net loss of 54,294 members a year over the next ten years.[66] With this loss of members some were losing trust that the Division of Evangelism was part of the solution. In September 1971, a Celebration of Evangelism was held in Cincinnati featuring many pastors identified with evangelism from both major branches of Presbyterianism. The Division of Evangelism declined to participate, but Peters attended through the urging of the PCUS pastor John Anderson. This event proved to be both a celebration and a caucus over future strategy. The celebration was mentioned in one sentence in the General Assembly report of 1972. Many who were doing evangelism locally felt increasingly cut off from those responsible for evangelism at the national level.[67]

General Assembly staffing in evangelism fluctuated greatly in these years. From 1966 through 1973 the staff varied from six full-time members to two full-time persons with one part-timer. By 1970, when the Church and Society report to the Assembly was 115 pages, the report of the Division of Evangelism had shrunk to five pages.[68]

In the early 1970s the program of Risk Evangelism was created by the Synod of the Trinity. The theological foundations of Risk were rooted in the theology of the Dutch theologian J. C. Hoekendijk.

Hoekendijk spoke of witness as embracing three components: *koinōnia* (life together), *diakonia* (deed or service), and *kērygma* (proclamation). Risk was a holistic attempt to hold word and deed together at this time when the word "evangelism" was suspect. In short order it was adopted by the UPCUSA evangelism office. It was promoted among PCUS churches as well. Year one focused on building up congregational life. Year two emphasized service to the community. Year three stressed traditional efforts to share the faith with those outside. Risk generated widespread enthusiasm but evaluations indicated that congregations tended to run out of steam in year three.[69]

A NEW CHURCH AND
NEW POSSIBILITIES

The reuniting of the PCUSA and the PCUS in Atlanta in 1983 to form the Presbyterian Church (U.S.A.) brought hope for new life in a Presbyterian tradition where the rank and file had become increasingly distrustful of national structures. The new church moved its offices to Louisville, Kentucky. The move from New York and Atlanta to Louisville, symbolized another part of a new beginning. A church structure was announced in 1987 that included a unit on Evangelism and Church Growth and one on Social Justice and Peacemaking. In truth, other units, such as a Racial Ethnic Ministry Unit and a Women's Ministry Unit, whose predecessor units would have seen evangelism as a primary task, now conceived of their task in terms of social witness. In addition, a Committee on Social Witness Policy was also put in place.

In 1988, Gary Demarest was appointed Associate for Evangelism. Demarest was a well-known pastor who had been a leader at both the Cincinnati Celebration of Evangelism (1971) and the Presbyterian Congress on Renewal (1985) and also served on the controversial Task Force on Central America. Some regarded his appointment as a sign that the national church could once again attract leadership in evangelism from persons who were recognized by their peers as ministers and evangelists rather than as managers.

At the reuniting Assembly in 1983 the Advisory Council on Church and Society (UPCUSA) and the Council on Theology and

Culture (PCUS) presented a substantive document titled "Reformed Faith and Politics." This work sought to lay the biblical, theological, and historical foundation for Presbyterian involvement in social, political, economic, and racial issues. Recognizing the objections among many Presbyterians, the report's history section began by saying, "Presbyterian resistance to the church acting in society is rooted in ignorance of Presbyterian history." The "Political Vocation of Presbyterians," it argued, is rooted in both "a comprehensive, complex social ethic that is demonstrated in the social teachings of each General Assembly" and a commitment to "the idea of worldly vocations."[70]

The Presbyterian Church (U.S.A.) came into being as the membership figures continued the drumbeat of an annual decline. Voices from many quarters spoke up to lobby for more emphasis on evangelism. By now the new or accompanying words were "church growth." Evangelism and church growth were not the same thing, but many Presbyterians gravitated to theories of church growth as a remedy for declining membership. The 1982 UPCUSA Assembly appointed a Special Committee on Evangelism and Church Growth.[71] As a direct result of this momentum the 1988 General Assembly adopted the Task Force on Church Membership Growth's call for each presbytery and session to adopt a Commitment to Evangelism. The special committee sought to address the polarization in the church over evangelism and justice. Reporting in 1984, the committee declared: "Far from being polarized from social responsibility, evangelism as central to the calling of the church gives meaning to social responsibility, and social responsibility gives meaningful expression to evangelism."[72]

Undergirding Presbyterian efforts to hold evangelism and social witness together was the report "Mission and Evangelism: An Ecumenical Affirmation." Adopted in 1983 by the World Council of Churches Assembly at Vancouver, its call to both proclamation and witness in this document was utilized extensively for guidance by various units of the new church.

Another initiative to restore evangelism to a priority in the church, however, caught everyone off guard at the 1990 General Assembly. A commissioner from the Presbytery of Central Florida offered the overture: "Resolved that General Assembly reaffirm its commitment to evangelism as a top priority." The overture instructed the General Assembly Council to affirm this priority by an annual increase to the Evangelism and Church Development Ministry of "one percent (1%) of the total General Assembly Mission Budget for a period of five years beginning in 1990."[73]

The Assembly was in an uproar. Staff advised that the budget was a pie that only could be shaped in certain ways, and the question was asked, Did the vote on the overture mean "if" the money could be raised? A suggestion was made to make the money part of the Bicentennial Fund. The overture passed, but the change in priority has never been fully funded.

When evangelism and justice were announced as the mission priorities for the 1990s, the General Assembly wanted to discover how these priorities related to each other. A two-stage process was planned. In November 1990 thirteen congregations were selected that had demonstrated that they were doing both evangelism and justice well. Taken together the congregations represented the geographical, ethnic, cultural, and theological diversity of the church. Gathering in Louisville with selected representatives from the church, including members from both the Evangelism and Church Development Unit and the Social Justice and Peacemaking Unit, the congregations told their stories to one another. Their conversation focused on discerning what characteristics distinguished vital congregations that were involved in both evangelism and justice ministries.[74]

These thirteen congregations became the keynote speakers for a 1991 pre-Assembly event in Baltimore. Participants were asked to reflect on personal and parish journeys as well as the larger story of the denomination in both evangelism and justice. The responses evoked both the complementary and sometimes competitive relationship of the two priorities. Biblical and theological motifs were probed as foundations for present ministries. Finally, participants worked together on metaphors and strategies for future evangelism and justice ministries.[75]

CONCLUSION

This story shows that several factors were pivotal in the changing definitions and strategies of both evangelism and social witness in this century.

Leadership was clearly critical. From Chapman to Sweazey, evangelism recruited recognized pastors who were evangelists. With the bureaucratization of the church, the norm by the 1950s, it became more difficult to recruit pastors who did not simply want to be managers. Moreover, the paradigm of a Chapman and a Stelzle working together was increasingly replaced by specialists in each aspect of the witness.

This division in leadership reflected a similar shift in program. As evangelism became suspect, a division grew up between outreach by word and by deed. This trend reached its zenith in the UP-CUSA's redefinition of evangelism in 1967, a statement that drove a wedge between evangelism and mission.

Structure likewise proved a key factor at the national level in shaping policy and strategy. The restructuring of the 1920s, 1970s, and 1980s affected the status and relationship of evangelism and social witness. The effect, especially in 1923, was not always intentional. It can be argued that evangelism was diminished and social witness grew in the reorganizations of the 1970s and 1980s.[76] Knowing these effects of restructuring should make the church look carefully at the implications for evangelism and social witness in any future restructurings.

Finally, the most pervasive distinction that has been effected since the 1960s is that between word and deed. Even in the midst of genuine attempts to combine evangelism and social justice in specific ministries, the assumption remains that evangelism is word and social witness is deed. This distinction may simply reflect a reticence on the part of most Presbyterians, including the clergy, to speak about their faith. The separation probably is present because many committed to social witness harbor suspicions based on past associations with evangelism.

In the reunited church there is evidence of many congregations engaged in creative ministries of evangelism and social witness. To do either well requires dedication, stamina, and time. To do both together demands both vision and energy.

Hopefully, present-day Presbyterians and Reformed church people can learn from the past. Evangelism and social witness have been both complementary and competitive in the Presbyterian story during the twentieth century. To understand their relationship is to be open to both insights and unsettled questions intersecting the present from the past. As these insights are appropriated and the questions addressed, Reformed Christians may discover a mutually enriching relationship between evangelism and social witness that will benefit the whole church of Jesus Christ.

NOTES

1. Presbyterian Church (U.S.A.), General Assembly, *Minutes,* 1990, Part I, 322. (Hereafter cited as PC(USA), GA, *Minutes.*)
2. Presbyterian Church in the United States of America, General Assembly, *Minutes,* 1818, 28–29. (Hereafter cited as PCUSA, GA, *Minutes.*)
3. Lefferts A. Loetscher, *A Brief History of the Presbyterians,* 4th ed. (Philadelphia: Westminster Press, 1983), 94; Andrew E. Murray, *Presbyterians and the Negro—A History* (Philadelphia: Presbyterian Historical Society, 1966), 63–102.
4. John Wilbur Chapman had distinguished himself as a pastor at Bethany Presbyterian in Philadelphia, where the Sunday school was led by the merchant John Wanamaker. It was said that the church in all its departments reached twelve thousand persons. In the 1890s Chapman became a nationally known evangelist, doing some work with Dwight L. Moody. The biographical information that follows comes from John Ramsay, *John Wilbur Chapman* (Boston: Christopher Publishing House, 1962); and Vincenta Stahmer, "John Wilbur Chapman: A Case Study in Presbyterian Evangelism" (M.Div. paper, Fuller Theological Seminary, 1990).
5. PCUSA, GA, *Minutes,* 1902, Part I, 38.
6. Elizabeth Osborn Thompson, ed., *Charles Lemuel Thompson: An Autobiography* (New York: Fleming H. Revell Co., 1924).
7. Ibid., 152.
8. See Charles Stelzle, *A Son of the Bowery* (New York: George H. Doran Co., 1926); Ronald C. White, Jr., and C. Howard Hopkins, *The Social Gospel: Religion Reform in Changing America* (Philadelphia: Temple University Press, 1976), 51–54, 65–68.
9. PCUSA, GA, *Minutes,* 1910, Part II, 25–26.
10. Ibid., 157.
11. PCUSA, GA, *Minutes,* 1910, Part I, 229–33.
12. Dale E. Soden, "Anatomy of a Presbyterian Urban Revival: J. W. Chapman in the Pacific Northwest," *American Presbyterians* 64 (spring 1986): 49–57.
13. Ramsay, *Chapman,* 130–31.
14. Elizabeth Osborn Thompson, *Charles Lemuel Thompson,* 159.
15. Ernest Trice Thompson, *Presbyterians in the South* (Atlanta: John Knox Press, 1973), vol. 3, 33, 36–37.

16. Ibid., 40–42; Milton J Coalter, "Presbyterian Evangelism: A Case of Parallel Allegiances Diverging," in *The Diversity of Discipleship: Presbyterians and Twentieth-Century Christian Witness,* ed. Milton J Coalter, John M. Mulder, and Louis B. Weeks (Louisville, Ky.: Westminster/John Knox Press, 1991), 37–38.

17. James Henley Thornwell, "The Relation of the Church to Slavery," in *The Collected Writings of James Henley Thornwell* (Edinburgh: Banner of Truth Trust, 1974; original publication 1875), vol. 4, 385.

18. "Address to the General Assembly," in ibid., 449; Ernest Trice Thompson, *Presbyterians in the South,* vol. 2, 30.

19. White and Hopkins, *Social Gospel,* 83, 85; Ernest Trice Thompson, *Presbyterians in the South,* vol. 3, 242–43.

20. Presbyterian Church in the United States, General Assembly, *Minutes,* 1908, 19 (hereafter cited as PCUS, GA, *Minutes*); Ernest Trice Thompson, *Presbyterians in the South,* vol. 3, 243.

21. PCUSA, Board of Home Missions, *Minutes,* 1906, Part II, 7; PCUSA, GA, *Minutes,* 1922, Part III, 7; Board of Home Missions, *Minutes,* GA, PCUSA, 1924, Part II, 43. Other statements that speak to the primacy of evangelism include PCUSA, GA, *Minutes,* 1915, Part II, 7; PCUSA, GA, *Minutes,* 1917, Part II, 12; PCUSA, GA, *Minutes,* 1925, Part I, 35, 75; PCUSA, GA, *Minutes,* 1927, Part II, 10.

22. PCUS, GA, *Minutes,* 1918, 8; PCUS, GA, *Minutes,* 1932, 49.

23. Alan Trachtenberg, *The Incorporation of America: Culture and Society in the Gilded Age* (New York: Hill & Wang), 3–4. See also Robert H. Wiebe, *The Search for Order, 1877–1929* (New York: Hill & Wang, 1967); Samuel Haber, *Efficiency and Uplift: Scientific Management in the Progressive Era, 1890–1920* (Chicago: University of Chicago Press, 1964); and Samuel P. Hays, *Conservation and the Gospel of Efficiency: The Progressive Conservation Movement, 1890–1920* (New York: Atheneum Publishers, 1975).

24. Louis B. Weeks, "The Incorporation of the Presbyterians," in *The Organizational Revolution: Presbyterians and American Denominationalism,* ed. Milton J Coalter, John M. Mulder, and Louis B. Weeks (Louisville, Ky.: Westminster/John Knox Press, 1992), 37, 43.

25. Ibid., 59.

26. Board of Home Missions, *Minutes,* GA, PCUSA, 1924, Part II, 43.

27. Coalter, "Presbyterian Evangelism," 39.

28. Ibid., 40–41. Robert T. Handy has referred to this phenomenon as a "religious depression."

29. Ibid., 63–64.

30. Reinhold Niebuhr, *Moral Man and Immoral Society* (New York: Charles Scribner's Sons, 1932), 81.

31. "Report of the Committee on Moral and Social Welfare," in Synod of Virginia, *Minutes,* 1933, 272–80.

32. Ernest Trice Thompson, *Presbyterians in the South,* vol. 3, 508.

33. PCUS, GA, *Minutes,* 1933, 30. I am indebted to James M. Singleton, Jr., for sharing with me research in progress for a D.Min. dissertation on evangelism in the PCUS.

34. Ernest Trice Thompson, *Presbyterians in the South,* vol. 3, 507.

35. Quoted in ibid., 174.

36. Ibid., 186.

37. Ibid., 188–90.

38. Ernest Trice Thompson, *Presbyterians in the South,* vol. 3, 508–9.

39. PCUS, GA, *Minutes,* 93.

40. Ibid., 94.

41. It is not always easy to keep up with the changing names of committees. In 1936 a new Standing Committee on Moral Welfare was authorized. In 1937 the name of the committee was changed to Social Education and Action. To help in understanding the tradition of social concern a document was prepared chronicling the "Official Pronouncements of the General Assembly Relative to Social and Industrial Relations and Social and Moral Welfare, 1910–1936," in the PCUSA, GA, *Minutes,* 1937, Part I, 214.

42. PCUSA, GA, Minutes, 1930, Part I, 109–10; PCUSA, GA, *Minutes,* 1931, Part I, 99, 101.

43. PCUSA, GA, *Minutes,* 1932, Part I, 126.

44. PCUSA, GA, *Minutes,* 1936, Part I, 154.

45. I acknowledge the insights and information in the unpublished paper by Thomas C. Berg, "'Proclaiming Together'? From Convergence to Divergence in Mainline and Evangelical Evangelism, 1945–67," *Religion and American Culture,* (forthcoming).

46. Board of National Missions, PCUSA, GA, *Minutes,* 1946, Part II, 12; PCUSA, GA, *Minutes,* 1948, Part I, 167.

47. PCUSA, GA, *Minutes,* 1950, Part I, 200.

48. Ibid., 202.

49. George E. Sweazey, *Effective Evangelism: The Greatest Work in the World* (New York: Harper & Brothers, 1953), 33–34, cited in Berg, "'Proclaiming Together'?" (forthcoming).

50. Coalter, "Presbyterian Evangelism," 43.

51. PCUSA, GA, *Minutes,* 1952, Part I, 170.

52. Coalter, "Presbyterian Evangelism," 45–46.

53. *Manual on a Mission of Christian Action* (Atlanta: Division of Evangelism, PCUS, n.d.), 3. There is no author given, but Singleton believes it was written by Albert E. Dimmock.

54. See Reinhold Niebuhr, "Literalism, Individualism, and Billy Graham," *Christian Century,* 73 (May 23, 1956): 640–41; Editorial, "Fundamentalist Revival," *Christian Century,* 74 (June 19, 1957): 749–51; cited in Berg, "'Proclaiming Together'?" (forthcoming).

55. Elmer G. Homrighausen, "Billy Graham and the Protestant

Predicament," *Christian Century,* 73 (July 18, 1956): 848–49; cited in Berg, "'Proclaiming Together'?" (forthcoming).

56. United Presbyterian Church in the United States of America, GA, *Minutes,* 1958, 526, 538–39. (Hereafter cited as UPCUSA, GA, *Minutes.*)

57. UPCUSA, GA, *Minutes,* 1965, 398–439; UPCUSA, GA, *Minutes,* 1967, 320–95; UPCUSA, GA, *Minutes,* 1970, 879–994; UPCUSA, GA, *Minutes,* 1972, 386–601.

58. UPCUSA, GA, *Minutes,* 1968, 385.

59. UPCUSA, GA, *Minutes,* 1980, Part I, 200–13.

60. UPCUSA, GA, *Minutes,* 1964, 220.

61. UPCUSA, GA, *Minutes,* 1966, 333.

62. Ibid., 334.

63. UPCUSA, GA, *Minutes,* 1967, Part I, 222.

64. UPCUSA, GA, *Minutes,* 1968, Part I, 292; Coalter, "Presbyterian Evangelism," 49.

65. UPCUSA, GA, *Minutes,* 1969, 647–51.

66. Milton J Coalter, John M. Mulder, Louis B. Weeks, eds., *The Re-Forming Tradition: Presbyterians and Mainstream Protestantism* (Louisville, Ky.: Westminster/John Knox Press, 1992), 152.

67. UPCUSA, GA, *Minutes,* 1972, 654.

68. UPCUSA, GA, *Minutes,* 1970, 874.

69. I am indebted to John R. Hendrick for the information and insights in this paragraph.

70. PC(USA), GA, *Minutes,* 1983, Part I, 772, 777.

71. UPCUSA, GA, *Minutes,* 1982, Part I, 85.

72. PC(USA), GA, *Minutes,* 1984, 129.

73. PC(USA), GA, *Minutes,* 1990, 62, 1018.

74. PC(USA), GA, *Minutes,* 1991, 481, 636.

75. The author of this chapter was privileged to be the General Assembly's Theological Consultant for both of these convocations.

76. An important facet not included in this chapter is budgets. It finally became too difficult to assess accurately how much money was spent on evangelism and social witness. This researcher has discovered that there are deep pockets in Presbyterian budgets. One cannot look simply at the unified budget, but at special bequests. In this sense the budgets for social witness are far larger than the budget for Social Justice and Peacemaking because other units often see their tasks as social witness.

Part 3. Groundwork for Future Witness

8. Locating a Reformed Theology of Evangelism in a Pluralistic World

DARRELL L. GUDER

The title of this essay is, so to speak, its assignment. I was asked to review the other essays in this project, and then, if possible, "to locate a Reformed theology of evangelism," based on these studies of Reformed theology and the North American Presbyterian case history within the Reformed tradition. The works cited most often will, therefore, be the other essays in this project.

When the Presbyterians just discussed in the previous three essays talked theology, they liked to speak of themselves as "Reformed." When they talked about how they organized themselves, about their polity, they used terms like "Presbyterian" or "Congregational." The essays in this project permit us, I believe, to talk *theologically* about evangelism, with the particular slant produced by the distinctive characteristics of the Presbyterian experience in America. That experience has, in the twentieth century, been characterized by a troubled relationship with evangelism, however defined. Thus, if one assigned a subtitle to this essay, it might be "The Presbyterian Problem with a Reformed Theology of Evangelism," or perhaps more neutrally, "The Presbyterian Agenda for a Reformed Theology of Evangelism."

The operative word in this essay, however, is *locating*. By that, I mean "finding the appropriate place for a theology of evangelism, or for integrating evangelism into the Reformed theological context." It is tempting, of course, to understand "locating" as "finding something which is lost," since it is not easy to find a Presbyterian *theology* of evangelism in our more recent history. The essays generally reveal that when Presbyterians talked about evangelism in the last sixty to seventy years, they tended to dwell on more methodological understandings of evangelism: evangelism as membership recruitment, or church planting, or church development. It would be hard to find much serious theological work on evangelism among Presbyterians before very recent years. Of course, if we were to understand that the fundamental issue is the theological question of our mission as the church, we would find that there is lively discussion going on around the world. Reformed missiologists (students of the church's mission) are particularly active in this discussion![1]

At the beginning of the century the situation with regard to evangelism was very different from now. As Louis Weeks has shown, there was a broad consensus in American Presbyterianism by the end of the Civil War that can be appropriately described as evangelical, namely, faith in Jesus Christ as the way, the truth, and the life for all humanity; the conviction that the scriptures are trustworthy and authoritative; and a commitment to gospel proclamation as the "primary duty of individual Christians and of the church."[2] Presbyterians agreed that evangelism was "telling the good news of a Saviour to the dying heathen,"[3] and most (not all!) Presbyterians were comfortable with the American revivalist variation of that definition, evangelism as "soul winning," or "leading a person to Christ."

THE PEDIGREE OF "EVANGELISM"
IN REFORMED CIRCLES

The term *evangelism* is not an old one in our tradition. It does not appear in the *Book of Confessions* until the Confession of 1967,[4] and there it is not defined. The Heidelberg Catechism speaks of "winning our neighbors to Christ" through our reverent behavior[5] as the explanation for the importance of good works. We may assume that the "neighbors" meant here, in the setting of the sixteenth century, were not pagans, but Catholics or others who needed to experience the true gospel in its Reformed restatement. The latter Catherine González calls the Reformers' "nominal Christian neighbors."[6]

In 1903, when the Presbyterian Church in the United States of America (PCUSA) added to the Westminster Confession of Faith Chapter XXXV, "Of the Gospel of the Love of God and Missions," it never mentioned evangelism, although it spoke of the church's mandate to go into all the world to make disciples of all nations.[7] The focus was clearly on *foreign* mission, however, with the expectation that "believers" here at home "are . . . under obligation to sustain the ordinances of the Christian religion where they are already established, and to contribute by their prayers, gifts, and personal efforts to the extension of the Kingdom of Christ throughout the whole earth."[8] Evangelistic mission was clearly understood then within the context of "already established" Christendom. It was an activity beyond our own national boundaries, in spite of more than two centuries of struggle with the disintegrating of traditional notions of Christendom in North America, which we looked back upon when we optimistically entered this "Christian century."[9]

There are understandable historical reasons for this contemporary Presbyterian hesitancy with the term "evangelism." The term "mission" or "missions" had a similar struggle before making its way into the Westminster Confession almost a century ago. The Reformed community has most often spoken of the proclamation of the word rather than evangelism, and we have meant by that, the gospel. However, as Albert Winn points out, we seldom used that word "gospel" in an evangelistic sense in traditional Reformed language![10] The enterprise of evangelism has been carried on within Christendom, that is, within a culture long since Christianized. The gospel has not been "new" news for our society. Its contents have been woven into the fabric of our public and private lives for centuries. The Reformed (as well as the Lutheran) tradition has been concerned about the correct preaching of the scriptural word with authority and discipline, normally done in the church by its authorized ministers. The Heidelberg Cathechism discusses the preaching of the holy gospel under the theme, "the office of the keys," and the clear context is the church's ministry within a Christian culture, where unbelief is understood as movement away from the standard and accepted tradition.[11]

It is worth remembering that the Reformation churches, both Lutheran and Reformed, initially resisted the idea of a missionary movement going beyond the boundaries of Christian Europe. In her essay, Catherine González summarizes helpfully the reasons for the slow emergence of a concept and practice of mission and evangelism within the Christian West.[12] So, what we may define as evangelism was implicitly going on every Sunday in every Reformed church pulpit, where the gospel was being proclaimed in the sermon.[13] However, as Reformed church people moved into the twentieth century, our Reformed assumptions about our evangelical centeredness began to be challenged from two directions.

On the home front the church confronted the new fact of the rapid secularization of European Christian culture when transplanted to America, what I just called the "disintegrating of traditional notions of Christendom in North America." A part of this process was the complex development we call disestablishment, or the gradual shift of Christianity from its dominant, privileged, and protected position within society to a much more marginal role. This shift proceeded slowly, but by now it seems fairly well in place, with the result that Christianity is largely consigned to the private realm of religion.

Although the various migrating cultural groupings brought their churches, their theologies, and even their church architecture with them from Europe, they did not necessarily retain their people when they crossed the Atlantic. Many who left Europe with their names on parish rolls did not automatically seek out new rolls on which to enter their names when they arrived here. They left a system of established Christianity, what Lamin Sanneh has well described as "territorial Christianity,"[14] and they entered, after the early years of our colonial period, a totally new kind of ecclesiastical reality on these shores: voluntary churches and the option not to belong. This meant, of course, that they were not in churches on Sunday mornings, hearing the gospel proclaimed. Although the churches continued to evangelize inside their walls, they did not reach vast numbers of the population outside their walls.

As Edith Blumhofer points out, Reformed churches struggled with this new challenge, as testified to in the Presbyterian Old School–New School controversies, and they responded to the challenge with a variety of strategies.[15] The Great Awakenings, revivalism, home mission societies, the Sunday school movement, literature, missions, and, in the twentieth century, parachurch organizations were all responses to this fundamental fact that the church in America does not automatically have a privileged relationship to all the people within its territory. To make matters more complex, there is no *one* church in any part of the American territory, but rather a divided church addresses a fragmented and secularized society. The European soil out of which we Protestants have grown has not prepared us theologically for the task of living in this environment.

The crucial issue for us, internationally, was, of course, the missionary movement. The discovery of unbelieving peoples in the non-Western world resulted in the amazing response of Western missions. In a little more than two centuries, this has led to the establishment of Christian churches in virtually every culture of the world. As we should know, the European and North American churches are by now the numerical minority in world Christianity.[16]

The fact of rapidly expanding world missions in the last century forced the Presbyterian Church to take account of this amazing new development by adding Chapter XXXV, mentioned above, to the Westminster Confession. But this confessional statement was so totally imbedded in the thought categories of Christendom that, from today's perspective, its primary importance is that of a benchmark, an indication of the Western church's growing awareness that our understanding of our mission was rapidly becoming inadequate. Lefferts Loetscher described the process as "the broadening church,"[17] a theological broadening that has continued in this century without hesitation.

Our reality today is one of theological diversity, a chorus of theological emphases and directions that ideally are centered around our fundamental commitments as defined in Reformed confessional documents. As we move toward the end of the century, our diversity is described often as "pluralistic," which implies for many that we no longer can claim the centeredness that makes our diversity mutually enriching. In spite of what the confessional documents and the official statements of church bodies may say, this pluralism seems to emerge as a problem for a theology of evangelism, since it appears impossible to find a consensus that could define the evangelistic mission of such a pluralist church.

When we review the developments in mission and evangelism in the twentieth century, we find that a sense of disorientation with regard to evangelism and mission soon emerges, broadens, and deepens. What was to have been "the Christian century" in the West soon proved otherwise. The optimism with which this century began dissipated in the dismay caused by World War I, the emergence of one social and economic crisis after another in the so-called Christian West, and the accompanying sense of skepticism and self-questioning that began to pervade much of mainline Christianity. The consensus about evangelism was soon gone, leaving the location of a Reformed theology of evangelism either an urgent and difficult task or an abandoned enterprise.[18]

It has long been clear that the theme of evangelism makes Presbyterians and other Reformed Christians nervous. The theology of evangelism is not really recognized yet as a full-fledged member of the theological disciplines. We are not exactly sure where it fits, what credentials one needs to teach it, and how to relate it to the theological context. I suggest, that the problem that makes it hard to locate a Reformed theology of evangelism is the theological diversity, if not pluralism, that has established itself as our norm in this century.

IMPEDIMENTS TO A THEOLOGICAL
CONSENSUS ON EVANGELISM

Assuming now that we are talking about pluralism within the church, there is a spectrum of issues that effectively impede the development of a theological consensus within our church about our evangelistic task. Today, it is easier to agree about evangelistic methods, especially about what we do not think is appropriate, than it is to find consensus about the theological basis for evangelism.

The impediments are rather major in nature. Milton J Coalter, John M. Mulder, and Louis B. Weeks have set them out concisely in *The Re-Forming Tradition*.[19] The theological agenda of the church, they propose, must deal with these questions:[20]

1. Who is Jesus Christ?
2. What is the authority for the Christian life?
3. What can we hope for in a world that is increasingly paralyzed by both personal and communal despair?
4. Why, after all, is there a church—an ordered community of Christians?

5. What do we as Reformed Christians offer as our contribution to Christian life and witness?

Rather than rehearse what is already well summarized in their book, I would like to comment on the importance of some of these issues for locating a Reformed theology of evangelism.

Christology

It seems to me that the fundamental issue before us is Christology. Virgil Cruz, along with a broad spectrum of New Testament scholars, has stressed that the monotheism of the Old Testament is radically changed when the New Testament faith community confesses that Jesus Christ is Lord.[21] Easter and Pentecost empowered the church to become evangelistic, and the evangel was, as Albert Winn notes, not just the gospel that Jesus preached, but the good news about the Lord Jesus, about the Christ, about God's Son.

Martin Hengel recently summarized the twentieth-century debate about New Testament Christology in lectures delivered on a tour of several American theological faculties.[22] While affirming that Jesus was consciously and intentionally messianic in his ministry, Hengel pointed out that the dominant approach of New Testament scholarship in this century has replaced that view with the idea that a very creative and constructive early church created a messianic Jesus out of a remarkable human being who was a great prophet or wisdom teacher or moral example or a combination of these, but no more.[23] The implications of this critical revision of the kerygma have been massive in the church. Among the most obvious is the loss of a sense of mission, a reason to evangelize. When the kingdom of God is separated from the person, work, and presence of Christ, then the reign of God becomes a debatable program, a culturally conditioned agendum, one offer among many religious offers that may or may not make much sense in our world. The church becomes one helping agency among many, trying to be responsive to the needs of the world. What David Hester describes as the church's possible role in a "common language" that works toward structures that approach the experiences of justice and love that God hopes for all people becomes the maximal kerygma left to us.[24]

171

Ultimately, what happens in the theological study bears fruit in the pulpit. Raymond Brown recently wrote that "preaching is not really Christian unless it is rooted in Jesus Christ."[25] He then added a comment that is not directed only at the Reformed situation but certainly applies, "It is discouraging to hear sermons in Christian churches where, despite the value of the message, Jesus is scarcely mentioned." Given the widespread skepticism and confusion about the person and work of Jesus Christ, it is understandably difficult to locate a theology of evangelism!

There are many other powerful theological implications of modern christological revisioning, all aspects of the environment we call pluralism. As a result of the separation of the person and work of Christ from the agenda of the kingdom, Christian theology and ethical practice must necessarily become Pelagian or semi-Pelagian. It emphasizes the role of human activity in our salvation rather than our utter dependence on God's grace in Christ.[26] Thus, *we*, the church and individual Christians, are held responsible for the extension or building of the kingdom, language that the Bible never uses in relationship to the reign of God.[27] In scripture, the reign is something we receive or enter into.

Christian theology can even become pantheistic or panentheistic when, in current thought, we find theologies of creation that envision a creation that does not require redemption. Another version of this kind of separation drives a wedge between the incarnation and the atonement, making Jesus the embodiment of the person God wants us to be, but leaving out the salvific events that make that new kind of life real. There is, generally, a curious hesitancy in much of our theology today to deal with the cross and its centrality for the gospel and our evangelism.[28] It is clear that there is a broad spectrum of approaches to our theological task, a diversity of assumptions and questions that govern theological conclusions. Perhaps we need to begin asking the risky and difficult question about the appropriate boundaries of our pluralism.[29] Is there a point at which our pluralism moves beyond a healthy diversity and becomes so divisive that we cannot, with the best of efforts, locate a consensus for a theology of evangelism anymore? And if that point is near or has been reached, what do we do then? "The Christian community today must return from its boundaries to its own center. It must return to the gospel of Jesus Christ, turn afresh to the word of God in Holy Scripture."[30]

To illustrate the problem of our pluralism, let me place before you two definitions of evangelism. The Evangelism and Church Development Ministry Unit of the Presbyterian Church (U.S.A.) defined it with these words in 1991:

> Evangelism is joyfully sharing the Good News of the sovereign love of God and calling all people to repentance, to personal faith in Jesus Christ as Savior and Lord, to active membership in the church, and to obedient service in the world.[31]

In a recent book that describes our pluralistic theological situation as "Theological Worlds," W. Paul Jones attempts to lay out schematically ways of "understanding the alternative rhythms of Christian Belief." Jones defines evangelism in this way:

> The evangelistic thrust of [the] church will focus upon identifying the meaning-world by which each person's living is already being defined, often unconsciously and thus unacknowledged. . . . Whatever functions as one's ultimate concern in this endeavor provides the content designatable as one's God.[32]

Locating a theology of evangelism on the spectrum represented by those definitions is no mean challenge for us!

One possible pathway toward a theology of evangelism could be the project proposed by the first question raised by Coalter, Mulder, and Weeks, "Who is Jesus Christ?" As we grapple with that issue (and we have wonderful theological resources with which to do it), we will then find ourselves compelled to examine the issue of evangelism in terms of the evangel. As Albert Winn says, "If the Presbyterian Church should ever become interested again in theology, it would find solid theological grounds for an evangelism that embraces the evangel."[33] The encounter with Jesus must necessarily be the encounter with his life, teaching, death, resurrection, and enthronement.

All of this is, in the confession of the early church, the good news. To ask, Who is Jesus Christ? is to ask, What is the good news of and about Jesus Christ? This is the challenge Winn places before us in his excellent essay. He documents the ways in which the gospel has

173

ceased to function as good news. To get the evangel back into evangelism, we must discover what makes this news good.[34] The collapse of Christendom, the paradigm shift through which we are now going,[35] may well be the God-given opportunity for our own re-evangelization. Certainly this would be a quintessentially Reformed way of understanding our situation: What should *semper reformanda* (our process of "always being reformed") mean other than our own continuing, transforming encounter with the gospel of Jesus Christ, converting us so that we may be its instruments for the conversion of others? This is certainly what Dawn DeVries has suggested when she stresses that evangelism must continue within the church in order for it to happen through the church in the world.[36] The continuing conversion of the church is the presupposition for its evangelistic ministry.

The Division between
Proclamation by Word and Deed

Another impediment to the locating of a theology of evangelism that will result from grappling with the evangel in evangelism is the unholy division between word proclamation and deed proclamation, between evangelism and charity. Ronald White has shown in his essay how this has become the overarching problem of Presbyterianism in the twentieth century.[37] But its roots are also deep. By the end of the nineteenth century, as Louis Weeks points out, evangelism was moving from a central focus for all the church did, understood holistically, to one program among many, conducted by the incorporated denominational church.[38] The basic problem in this shift was the assumption that the mission of the gospel was twofold: verbal evangelistic proclamation and social ethical action. These were essentially different kinds of undertakings, with distinctive although related goals, different methods, and different constituencies. It was necessary, then, to formulate a social gospel. This social gospel, by its very name, implies that the definitions of the gospel that preceded it were perceived as inadequate.

In foreign missions, and especially in education, a similar problem was emerging. Education in other cultures was not proving to be evangelistically effective. Consequently, the mission of Christian educational institutions was redefined as contributing "to the good of the whole people rather than to the development of the Christian community or to the winning of members for the church," or as "leavening of non-Christian society and the relief of suffering."[39] Not long thereafter, denominational leaders began to criticize any intention to evangelize in other cultures.[40] This critique found its summarizing expression in the Hocking Report of the 1930s.[41] One way to redefine the enterprise and to overcome the dichotomy between verbal proclamation and deed proclamation was to call everything mission and thus to redefine evangelism in such a way that any form of activism for the common good fulfilled the definition.[42]

The reunited Presbyterian Church (U.S.A.) has sought to correct that trend by establishing two goals: "doing evangelism" and "doing justice." This positive step is also a candid admission that we are still struggling with our understanding of the evangel, so we divide it into parallel tracks, described it as the "two arms of the church," and we valiantly endeavor to relate these emphases. But we will not "locate a Presbyterian or Reformed theology of evangelism" until we have defined the gospel and our mission in a way that integrates these dimensions, until we know what it means "to do the gospel." Together with the christological challenge, this is a central impediment that must be overcome.

The Church and Its Mission

If the pathway to a theology of evangelism starts with our Christology, followed thereafter by a clarification of the gospel's integration of voice and limb in witness, then we are brought to the final major problem area for a theology of evangelism: the church and its mission.

Many might assume that a discussion of the theology of evangelism should be located within the theological discussion of the church's task and functions, what we call ecclesiology. By placing these questions here, after the central christological and gospel-definition questions, I am following the sober counsel of Ernst Käsemann, who has noted that "wherever ecclesiology moves into the foreground, however justifiable the reasons may be, Christology will lose its decisive importance, even if it does so by becoming integrated, in some form or other, in the doctrine of the church, instead of remaining the church's indispensable touchstone."[43]

It is appropriate then that the ecclesiological issue was the *fourth* question raised by Coalter, Mulder, and Weeks: Why is there a church? We should note, however, that the American discussion in these last decades has, for the most part, not put the question in quite such a rigorous way. The existence of the church has been assumed in typical Christendom style, and its problems have been analyzed in great detail. Using more sociological and anthropological approaches than ecclesiological, commentators have asked: Why is the church decreasing in membership?[44] How and why is it realigning?[45] Why do some kinds of churches grow while others do not?[46] What kinds of congregations function best for what purposes and why?[47]

We do not discern any consensus about the reason for the church, its mission. Here again, pluralism is part of the problem. My hunch is that our christological crisis has made it very difficult to develop any kind of consensus about the church. After all, we are not really sure Christ ever intended it to happen!

Yet the discussion about the church, on an international and ecumenical level, is a lively and helpful one. The new fact of the global church is informing the debate very productively. The churches of the West, still coming to terms with their centuries of establishment and cultural privilege and the subsequent loss of that privileged position, are having to go to school missiologically and learn from their partner churches in the non-Western world.

The global consensus is that "mission belongs to the essence of the church."[48] The *missio Dei* (the mission of God) defines the reason for the church's existence and action.[49] The whole world is a mission field, especially Western culture, which still likes to style itself as Christian or Judeo-Christian. The church is not an end in itself but God's elect instrument for God's purposes. Thus, the church's mission is essentially trinitarian, which David Bosch defines as "mediating the love of God the Father who is the Parent of all people, whoever and wherever they may be. It is epiphany, the making present in the world of God the Son. It is mediating the presence of God the Spirit, who blows where He wishes."[50] Missiology and ecclesiology thus merge, and out of this comprehensive theological context must emerge our theology of evangelism.

Bosch, echoing the constant theme of Lesslie Newbigin these last decades, states:

> Just as the church ceases to be church if it is not missionary, theology ceases to be theology if it loses its missionary character. The crucial question, then, is not simply or only or largely what church is or what mission is; it is also what theology is and is about. We are in need of a missiological agenda for theology rather than just a theological agenda for mission, for theology, rightly understood, has no reason to exist other than critically to accompany the missio Dei. So mission should be "the theme of all theology." Missiology may be termed the "synoptic discipline" within the wider encyclopaedia of theology.[51]

As a "synoptic discipline," a study that relates all the themes of Christian teaching to one another, missiology thus claims to be *the* integrative theological discipline.

THE LOCUS OF EVANGELISM
FOUND IN THE MISSION OF GOD

If the *missio Dei,* the mission of God, is the theme of all theology, then we have arrived, I think, at the central locus of the Reformed understanding of revealed truth: the creative, self-disclosing, saving, and sending God of the biblical witness. And if our chief end is to glorify God, then our understanding of what that means must necessarily focus on God's mission, what it is that God is doing in God's creation, and our role as God's people in that action. I would suggest that this is the place to locate our theology of evangelism. This is where the biblical witness leads us.

Donald Gowan has found the "foundation of all evangelistic work" to be the "doctrine of God which insists there is but one God, to whom all the peoples of the earth are responsible."[52] Arlo Duba and Joyce Tucker, similarly, have identified the theological foundation of evangelism in the very nature of God as a sending God, with the overarching biblical assertion that the creation belongs to God and is called to give glory to the Creator. In their words, "the triune, sending God revealed in Jesus Christ is the source of all witness and mission, as well as the focus of worship."[53]

The God of the biblical witness is the loving Redeemer God, the "sending God," the "outreaching God," the Father of our Lord Jesus Christ. This is very good news. What the Bible says about the character of God and God's action is gospel from the first page to the last page. God is not against us. God's justifiable anger with our sin is not God's final word. God has always been about salvation, has always desired reconciliation and the restoration of the lost creation. God's judgment does not contradict God's grace; at the cross, both merge and grace is triumphant. When Paul starts his great exposition of the gospel, he calls it the "gospel of God." He says that, as a servant of Jesus Christ, he is "called to be an apostle, set apart for the gospel of God, which he promised beforehand through his prophets in the holy scriptures, the gospel concerning his Son." (Rom. 1:1–3).

God's sovereign actions in history are good news, and to celebrate that good news as its evangelists is to glorify God. This sovereign loving God is at work in our history, our experience, to bring about the healing and salvation of the world. God's infinite power is directed toward us in our finiteness, to bring us to new life, to hope, to faith.

This certainty has been at the heart of Reformed teaching since Calvin constantly emphasized it in all his teaching and writing in Geneva. It is the marrow of the Reformed and Presbyterian understanding of evangelism. Merwyn Johnson summarizes Calvin's understanding of God's sovereignty in evangelism this way: "According to Calvin's view of grace, God alone saves, and God alone does the work of evangelism. Grace proclaims the redeeming presence and activity of *God* in our midst. Our relationship with God is alive and valuable for its own sake, because *God* is alive, active, and gracious."[54]

It would be fair to say, as several of the essayists affirm, that this high view of the gospel as good news about the character and action of God was the ground and message of Reformed and Presbyterian churches through most of their history. It may not have been called evangelism. We may not have understood our Reformed theological enterprise as a theology of evangelism. There may even have been some ways in which we have interpreted the gospel that obscured its goodness, but the essence of the Reformed understanding of the gospel is inherently evangelistic, if we are to glorify God through our life and worship and service.

Yet, as we have seen, the issues with which we have struggled in this century have made us self-critical, perhaps unsure of ourselves, and cautious in our assertions. Given the triumphalism of our gospel proclamation in earlier centuries, this has been an important corrective. Some of our reserve regarding evangelism has to do with reactions to much that has happened in our culture under the rubric "evangelism" that we cannot sanction: manipulation, emotionalism, cultural imperialism, individualism. These questionable methods of evangelism have made us hesitant about the enterprise.

Our history, our theological diversity becoming divisive pluralism, and especially the crises of the twentieth century, have also made us skeptics about evangelism. As we sorted out the trauma of World War I, many Christians began to feel that the church had been manipulated by the state for its purposes. The challenges of racism and economic injustice, the partnership between colonialism and mission, the encounter with other religions and the resulting questions about Christian claims to uniqueness, the religious skepticism that was the mark of the intellectual in the American university—all these and other issues led us to "lose our nerve" evangelistically, as Lamin Sanneh has put it.

But perhaps we may now emerge from this long bout of relativism, "corrosive pluralism," and agonizing self-appraisal and thankfully confess that we have learned that to be convinced of the truth of the gospel does not exclude a necessary modesty about ourselves as its witnesses and theological intepreters. As George Hunsberger has noted, "Our way of understanding God and putting the gospel can never be equated with the God who engages us and the message of God addressed to the whole of the world. Our grasp and experience are necessarily partial. They are historically and culturally framed."[55]

Chastened by this necessary learning, we may now locate our theology of evangelism in our theology of God, of God in Christ, of the gospel of Christ as the message of the reign of God both present and coming, and of the church as its messenger and witness.

FACTORS WORTHY OF ATTENTION
IN ANY THEOLOGY OF EVANGELISM

As we go about the task of locating and defining a Reformed theology of evangelism, we should give attention to these factors:

1. There is a rich vocabulary in the Old and New Testaments around the concept of witness that might emerge as the integral biblical concept for our theological formulations. Donald Gowan has pointed out that Yahweh works through Israel to make witness to God happen. In Ezekiel, we find the "beginnings of scripture's teaching that it is essential for non-believers to be able to see that the people of God are a faithful, loving community—the first kind of witness."[56] Virgil Cruz has added that the New Testament insists "that God's people are to witness to [God] especially by reflecting God's character in their own character and manner of life."[57] Jesus himself incarnates the reign of God, and his actions were "signs of the presence of the kingdom,"[58] which is the ministry we are to continue.[59] The word family of "witness" in the Lukan work defines the entire nature of both the individual and the corporate Christian presence in the world.[60] Our theology of evangelism would do well to build on this concept, which comprehends kērygma (the message proclaimed), koinōnia (the community), and diakonia (service).

2. As we develop our theology of evangelism, we must work especially hard to distinguish and to relate the individual and corporate dimensions of faith in Christ and of Christian discipleship. This is a recurring theme in the essays, and it arises surely out of our necessary struggle with the individualism of our Enlightenment culture and the privatism of American spirituality.[61] Conversion, as Dawn DeVries shows us, is both individual and corporate; and worship, as Duba and Tucker have noted, links the individual and the community especially around the table call.[62]

Our understanding of corporate witness may not be speechless, as the unholy dichotomy between word proclamation and deed proclamation has made it. But it must also not be disembodied word. As Donald Gowan has admonished us, "Without giving up our emphasis on proclamation, we must take with the utmost seriousness the necessity of maintaining or reestablishing the integrity of our Christian communities as places where hesed [mercy] . . . and agape [self-giving love] . . . are alive and visible, and to take this as an essential part of the work we call evangelism."63 We must learn to read the Bible with its plural "you"—the "ye" we lost when we gave up the King James Version!

3. Our theology of evangelism must focus the church on God's purpose for the world, the New Testament cosmos into which God sent the Son and for which Christ died (John 3). The church easily becomes an end in itself, just as the gospel easily becomes the way we each get the personal and individual benefits of salvation.64 But, as Dawn DeVries reminds us, conversion is not the only, or even the most important, task of the Christian church.65

This mighty work of God's love is purposeful; its intention is to draw people to the point where "they can participate in the work of realizing God's purposes for the whole creation."66 This is what David Hester emphasizes when he speaks of Christian "education for public transformation" and when he describes the church's mission as its "life of public witness."67 Similarly, Lesslie Newbigin and the Gospel and Our Culture Network, which has emerged from the discussion he initiated, call for a new articulation of the gospel as public truth.68

This is not a call for the reinstatement of Christendom. It is not a program for Christian power brokering in the public marketplace, whereby the church reveals its own bondage to the culture into which it is sent as Christ's witness. It is the claim that the gospel is not private but public, not passive but active, not hidden but displayed in the life, action, and language of the Christian community. The gospel as public truth challenges the idols and gods that dominate the public sphere. Thus, this witness is a cross-bearing witness, for it may well find that rejection and even persecution ensue when it is clearly proclaimed.

4. Finally, we can only locate our theology of evangelism in a pluralist world if we agree that we begin and continue the process in attentive, critical, disciplined, and prayerful study of scripture. Lesslie Newbigin suggests that we must draw our life from an "indwelling" of the Bible, the extended encounter with scripture that will empower us "to read the culture in terms of the Bible, not the Bible in terms of the culture."69 Would it not make missiological

sense for us to look closely at the impact of the Bible study movement in the Korean Presbyterian Church and elsewhere in the third world, when we consider how we might go about developing a theology of evangelism at our Reformed grass roots? There is a constant need for us to rediscover the meaning of *sola scriptura* as a church once "Reformed and always reforming."

Locating a Reformed theology of evangelism is a missiological enterprise. Evangelism is what God's Spirit calls and equips us to do as the church, and the theology we develop must help us understand the nature of that calling and carry it out more faithfully. As David Bosch says, our "mission is, quite simply, the participation of Christians in the liberating mission of Jesus, wagering on a future that verifiable experience seems to belie. It is the good news of God's love, incarnated in the witness of a community, for the sake of the world."[70]

NOTES

1. Among the many possible citations, I refer only to the magisterial work by David Bosch, *Transforming Mission: Paradigm Shifts in Theology of Mission* (Maryknoll, N.Y.: Orbis Books, 1991), passim but esp. 409–20. The ecumenical discussion is well represented by *Mission and Evangelism: An Ecumenical Affirmation* (Geneva: World Council of Churches, 1983).

2. Louis B. Weeks, "'Proclaim a Pure Gospel': Presbyterian Outreach from the Civil War to the Present," 113.

3. Charles W. Forman, "Evangelism in Global Mission: The American Presbyterian Experience" (paper presented at the Faithful Witness Conference, Louisville Presbyterian Theological Seminary, Louisville, Ky., March 18–19, 1993), 4, quoting from the 1845 General Assembly of the Presbyterian Church U.S.A.

4. *The Constitution of the Presbyterian Church (U.S.A.), Part I: Book of Confessions* (Louisville, Ky.: Office of the General Assembly, 1991), 9.37.

5. Ibid., 4.086, Question 86.

6. Catherine Gunsalus González, "'Converted and Always Converting': Evangelism in the Early Reformed Tradition," 79.

7. *Book of Confessions*, 6.187–.190.

8. Ibid., 6.190. It is intriguing that the revisers of the Westminster Confession at the turn of the century addressed the issue of foreign missions but left out any reference to the phenomenon of home missions, evangelism in our own culture, revivals and adult conversions in our cities, in spite of the turbulent developments in this area in the preceding decades.

9. One is reminded of the optimism that led the noted American journal to adopt this name, *The Christian Century*, in 1900.

10. Albert Curry Winn, "What Is the Gospel?" 14–17.

11. *Book of Confessions*, 4.083, .084.

12. González, "'Converting and Always Converting,'" 74–78.

13. Arlo D. Duba and Joyce C. Tucker, "Preaching, Worship and Evangelization in the Presbyterian Church (U.S.A.) Tradition," 1 (paper presented at the Faithful Witness Conference, Louisville Presbyterian Theological Seminary, Louisville, Ky., March 18–19, 1993).

14. Dr. Lamin Sanneh discussed this theme in his address to the "Gospel as Public Truth" Conference, held in Swanwick, England, in July 1992.

15. Edith L. Blumhofer, "Awakenings to New Possibilities in Outreach: Evangelism in Pre-Civil War American Presbyterianism," 101–105.

16. David B. Barrett's computations for mid-1993 indicate that there are 994,339,000 Christian church members in the continents of Africa, East Asia, Latin America, Oceania, and South Asia; and 732,087,000 in Europe, European Asia/Eurasia, and North America. While the statistics should be revised with regard to Australia and New Zealand and Eurasia, the proportion will not change significantly.

17. Lefferts A. Loetscher, *The Broadening Church: A Study of Theological Issues in the Presbyterian Church since 1869* (Philadelphia: University of Pennsylvania Press, 1954), esp. chap. 10, "Revision Accomplished," 83ff.

18. See Milton J Coalter, "Presbyterian Evangelism: A Case of Parallel Allegiances Diverging," and John R. Fitzmier and Randall Balmer, "A Poultice for the Bite of the Cobra: The Hocking Report and Presbyterian Missions in the Middle Decades of the Twentieth Century," in *The Diversity of Discipleship: Presbyterians and Twentieth-Century Christian Witness*, ed. Milton J Coalter, John M. Mulder, and Louis B. Weeks (Louisville, Ky.: Westminster/John Knox Press, 1991), 33–54, 105–25.

19. Milton J Coalter, John M. Mulder, and Louis B. Weeks, *The Re-Forming Tradition: Presbyterians and Mainstream Protestantism* (Louisville, Ky.: Westminster/John Knox Press, 1992). This volume concludes the seven-volume research project titled The Presbyterian Presence: The Twentieth-Century Experience.

20. Ibid., 281–85.

21. Virgil Cruz, "How Christianity Became an Evangelistic Religion: A Survey of Some Pertinent New Testament Material," 2 (paper presented at the Faithful Witness Conference, Louisville Presbyterian Theological Seminary, Louisville, Ky., March 18–19, 1993).

22. I heard Martin Hengel, the distinguished Tübingen professor emeritus of New Testament, present his three lectures on the Messiahship of Jesus at Southern Baptist Theological Seminary in Louisville, Ky., March 4, 5, and 8, 1993.

23. Hengel pointed to Wilhelm Wrede's monograph *Das Messiasge-*

heimnis (1901) as the platform for most twentieth-century interpretation along these lines. See Stephen Neill, *The Interpretation of the New Testament, 1861–1961* (London: Oxford University Press, 1966), passim but especially 248ff., for a British commentary on this issue.

24. David C. Hester, "Evangelism and Education: Making Disciples Reformed," 64ff.

25. Raymond E. Brown, *A Once-and-Coming Spirit at Pentecost: Essays on the Liturgical Readings between Easter and Pentecost, Taken from the Acts of the Apostles and from the Gospel according to John* (Collegeville, Minn.: Liturgical Press), forthcoming; the quotation is from chapter 1.

26. Shirley C. Guthrie, "A Reformed Theology of Evangelism," in *Evangelism in the Reformed Tradition,* ed. Arnold B. Lovell (Decatur, Ga.: CTS Press, 1990), 76–80.

27. K. L. Schmidt, in his article on *basileia* in *Theological Dictionary of the New Testament,* ed. Gerhard Kittel and Gerhard Friedrich, trans. Geoffrey W. Bromiley (Grand Rapids: Wm. B. Eerdmans Publishing Co., 1964–1976), vol. 1, 581ff., emphasizes that the kingdom of God in the Synoptic Gospels is God's soteriological action for humankind, which is the central theme of Jesus' and his apostles' proclamation. The way into the kingdom is *metanoia,* (repentance). "The kingdom of God comes to us, and does so without any action on our part. . . . To want to bring about the kingdom by force is human arrogance, self-righteous Pharisaism, refined zealotry" (585). The kingdom is entered, given, promised, (585f.), but the human activity toward the kingdom is volitional: seeking, responding.

28. The otherwise excellent Presbyterian statement on evangelism, "Turn to the Living God: A Call to Evangelism in Jesus Christ's Way" (Louisville, Ky.: Office of the General Assembly, 1991), 7, does not speak about the cross when developing its theology of reconciliation; it is obviously implied.

29. My colleague George Hunsberger has pointed out that if we have a consensus about the center, then boundaries are less of a problem. I am aware of all the dangers linked with concern about the boundaries of pluralism, and thus in what follows I seek to focus on the issues at the center.

30. Paul McGlasson, *God the Redeemer: A Theology of the Gospel* (Louisville, Ky.: Westminster/John Knox Press, 1993), 12.

31. "Presbyterian Evangelism: Looking to the 21st Century" (Louisville, Ky.: Evangelism and Church Development Ministry Unit, Presbyterian Church (U.S.A.), 1991), 5, and in many other similar publications.

32. W. Paul Jones, *Theological Worlds: Understanding the Alternative Rhythms of Christian Belief* (Nashville: Abingdon Press, 1989), 12, 14.

33. Winn, "What Is the Gospel?" 22.

34. Ibid., 20–23.

35. Bosch, *Transforming Mission,* esp. 349ff.

36. Dawn DeVries, "What Is Conversion?" 39.

37. Ronald C. White, Jr., "Social Witness and Evangelism: Complementary or Competing Priorities?" 149ff.

38. Weeks, "'Proclaim a Pure Gospel,'" 129.

39. Forman, "Evangelism in Global Mission," 9.

40. Ibid.

41. See Fitzmier and Balmer, "Poultice for the Bite of the Cobra."

42. Weeks, "'Proclaim a Pure Gospel,'" 126.

43. Ernst Käsemann, *Perspectives on Paul* (Philadelphia: Fortress Press, 1971), 121–21; I am grateful to my colleague Marion Soards for bringing Käsemann's discussion on "the motif of the Body of Christ" to my attention.

44. See, e.g., Dean R. Hoge and David Roozen, eds., *Understanding Church Growth and Decline, 1950–1978* (New York: Pilgrim Press, 1979).

45. See, e.g., Robert Wuthnow, *The Restructuring of American Religion: Society and Faith since World War II* (Princeton, N.J.: Princeton University Press, 1988); Wade Clark Roof and William McKinney, *American Mainline Religion* (New Brunswick, N.J.: Rutgers University Press, 1984).

46. See, e.g., Dean M. Kelley, *Why Conservative Churches Are Growing* (San Francisco: Harper & Row, 1972).

47. See, e.g., James F. Hopewell, *Congregation: Stories and Structures,* ed. Barbara G. Wheeler (Philadelphia: Fortress Press, 1987); Jackson W. Carroll, Carl S. Dudley, and William McKinney, eds., *Handbook for Congregational Studies* (Nashville: Abingdon Press, 1986).

48. Bosch, *Transforming Mission,* 493

49. Ibid., 389ff.

50. Ibid., 493f.

51. Ibid., 494.

52. Donald E. Gowan, "How Christianity Became an Evangelistic Religion: Old Testament Evidence," 1 (paper presented at the Faithful Witness Conference, Louisville Presbyterian Theological Seminary, Louisville, Ky., March 18–19, 1993).

53. Duba and Tucker, "Preaching, Worship, and Evangelization," 2.

54. Merwyn Johnson, "Calvin's Significance for Evangelism Today" in *Calvin Studies V: Papers Presented to the Davidson Colloquium on Calvin Studies,* ed. John H. Leith, (Richmond, 1990), 119.

55. George Hunsberger, "Possessing a Peculiar Story: Recovering a Missionary Way of Living" (address for the Gospel and Our Culture Network Annual Meeting, Chicago, February 18, 1993), 5–6.

56. Gowan, "How Christianity Became an Evangelistic Religion," 2–8.

57. Cruz, "How Christianity Became an Evangelistic Religion," 10.

58. Winn, "What Is the Gospel?" 7–12.

59. See the definition of the ministry of God's people in "Ministry," chap. 7, *The COCU Consensus: In Quest of a Church of Christ Uniting,* 2d ed. (Princeton, N.J.: Consultation on Church Union, 1991), 40ff.

60. See Darrell L. Guder, *Be My Witnesses; The Church's Mission, Mes-*

sage, and Messengers (Grand Rapids: Wm. B. Eerdmans Publishing Co., 1985), passim, but especially 91ff.; see also the comprehensive discussion of the "witness" word family in Acts in chap. 4 of Marion Soards's forthcoming *The Speeches in Acts: An Appreciation of Their Contents, Context, and Concerns* (Louisville, Ky.: Westminster/John Knox Press, 1994).

    61. Among the many who are addressing this issue, Lesslie Newbigin is preeminent; see, for example, his *Foolishness to the Greeks: The Gospel and Western Culture* (Grand Rapids: Wm. B. Eerdmans Publishing Co., 1986), 21ff.

    62. Duba and Tucker, "Preaching, Worship and Evangelization."

    63. Gowan, "How Christianity Became an Evangelistic Religion."

    64. In Guder, *Be My Witnesses,* I describe this as the "mission-benefits dichotomy" at 226ff. and often elsewhere.

    65. DeVries, "What Is Conversion?" 40.

    66. Ibid.

    67. Hester, "Evangelism and Education," 64ff.

    68. Lesslie Newbigin, *Truth to Tell: The Gospel as Public Truth* (Grand Rapids: Wm. B. Eerdmans Publishing Co., 1991).

    69. Hunsberger, "Possessing a Peculiar Story," 10.

    70. Bosch, *Transforming Mission,* 519.